Digital Wealth

Digital Wealth

An Automatic Way to Invest Successfully

Simon Moore

WILEY

Published by John Wiley & Sons, Inc., Hoboken, New Jersey.
Published simultaneously in Canada.

For general information on our other products and services or for technical support, please
contact our Customer Care Department within the United States at (800) 762-2974, outside
the United States at (317) 572-3993 or fax (317) 572-4002.

Wiley publishes in a variety of print and electronic formats and by print-on-demand. Some
material included with standard print versions of this book may not be included in e-books or
in print-on-demand. If this book refers to media such as a CD or DVD that is not included in
the version you purchased, you may download this material at http://booksupport.wiley.com.
For more information about Wiley products, visit www.wiley.com.

Library of Congress Cataloging-in-Publication Data:

ISBN 9781119118466 (Hardcover)
ISBN 9781119118480 (ePDF)
ISBN 9781119118473 (ePub)

Printed in the United States of America

10 9 8 7 6 5 4 3 2 1

Dedicated to Mum and Dad.
Thank you for everything.

Contents

Preface

The future is already here. It's just not very evenly distributed.
—William Gibson

I n 1989, three separate global events heralded a revolution in household investing, with the potential to save American households billions over the coming decades.

In 1989, researchers from Carnegie Mellon University's ChipTest project joined forces with IBM. Their computer was renamed Deep Blue after a naming contest. This chess computer would ultimately defeat the world champion. The same principles of deep analysis and simulation across multiple scenarios are employed by investment algorithms. The technology that beat the world champion once required a room of computing power. Today, as a sign of the incredible improvements in processing power, that same software no longer requires its own room and can run on a basic consumer phone.

In May 1989, Index Participation Shares (IPS) began trading on the American and Philadelphia stock exchanges, an equity derivative attempting to match the returns of the Standard & Poor's (S&P) 500.[1] The Chicago Mercantile Exchange sued, and a decision by a Chicago Federal Court ultimately stopped the practice due to regulatory issues. But public interest in trading an entire stock market in the same way that you can trade a single stock was demonstrated in the brief period that this product traded.

The concept ultimately led to a similar fund being set up in Toronto to track the TSE-35 index the next year, which was again short lived, but this led to the first U.S. exchange-traded fund (ETF) four years later. These ETFs ultimately created a low-cost way to track all major liquid asset classes in a tax-efficient manner.

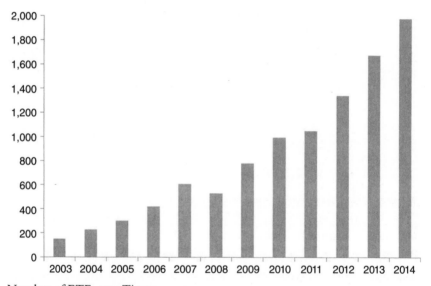

Number of ETFs over Time

Source: Investment Company Institute.

But the innovation was just as powerful in cost as in simplicity. At the turn of the millennium, the average mutual fund charged an expense ratio of 1.6 percent a year; now many ETFs have expense ratios of 0.1 percent or even lower. That represents a 93 percent decline in costs, often with other important benefits in ease of trading and tax efficiency, too.

And in 1989, Tim Beners Lee was in Switzerland pioneering the idea of hypertext to link different computers together. This was the early stages of the Internet. The Web has evolved in critical and unforeseen ways since then. This is the technology that enables investment advice to now be delivered online with tremendous efficiency. These benefits are shared with clients in the form of much lower cost and greater ease of access and implementation than with traditional investment practices.

This book explains how and why algorithmic investing works—how it builds on these three pivotal developments in recent decades spanning different fields. Computational analysis is well suited to large-scale number crunching, with the ability to perform calculations more accurately, frequently, and without error than humans. In addition to that discussion of what powers algorithmic investing, you will see how a low-cost approach and diversified approach to investing has historically led to better results and how this finding is supported by many academic studies. One major theme that research shows is how lower-cost investing typically provides superior results than more expensive strategies.

In turn, digital investment advice embodies decades of financial development including Nobel Prize–winning economic thinking. This book also explains the often overlooked area of tax-efficient investing and how the market's focus on pretax returns misses one of the easiest ways to improve performance. This is because beating the market is challenging given the competitive forces in play, yet tax efficiency offers a way to potentially increase portfolio returns in a more sustainable manner.

Unfortunately, today America's savings rate is too low for many and is well below historic norms. Many are still overpaying for investment advice or unintentionally mismanaging their own investment portfolio due to behavioral and other biases. This book explains what the future of investment management is likely to look like based on the tremendous growth of both ETFs as an asset class and digital investment advisors as an important service.

Investment advice has previously been the preserve of the wealthy, and digital advisors pose less of a threat to the traditional financial advisor and more of an opportunity for the field of financial advice to reach the majority of households who are managing their own portfolio. This shift should save countless households significant time and effort, while providing peace of mind on some of life's most important but often neglected topics.

---

[1] Gary L. Gastineau, *The Exchange-Traded Funds Manual*. Hoboken, NJ: Wiley, 2010.

Acknowledgments

T hanks to Jon and Bo for creating everything that this book documents—taking what was, at the time, a potentially radical and unproven idea and working tirelessly to make it appear obvious in retrospect. Thanks to Ephrat and the entire engineering team for algorithmic genius in converting finance into code, and Gary for his daily oversight and ideas. Thanks to Ed and Pawel for their design expertise. Thanks also to Mitch, Rob, Patrick, and Will for their unrelenting feedback on what I write every week. Thanks to Joe for making this happen, and to Sam, Jesse, and Chris for their early work and feedback on the concept. Thanks also to Casson for his data analysis and Huw for his cartoons. Thanks to Tula, Stacey, and the whole team at Wiley for their patience when deadlines weren't always met. Thanks to the whole team at FutureAdvisor, who make low-cost and high-quality financial services a reality for more and more people every day.

Thanks especially to Jamie for her support throughout the whole process. Thanks to Freddie, even though I'm aware that this book doesn't contain nearly enough pachycephalosauruses; and to Maggie, even though you would have much preferred a book with more pictures, especially ones of puppies.

Chapter 1

America's Savings Challenge

"The best time to plant a tree was 20 years ago; the second best time is now."

—Chinese Proverb

We Don't Save Enough

As many an NFL star can attest, it can be easy to have wealth in the short term but not keep it for the long term by spending beyond your long-term means. This problem plays out across U.S. society. The allure of advertising and broad availability of debt don't help. It can lead to a bias toward spending, rather than saving, to try and keep up with the neighbors. This often comes at the expense of long-term security.

Unfortunately, the numbers for savings rates in the United States are poor relative to both history and other countries. As you can see from Figure 1.1, up until the 1980s, the U.S. savings rate was comfortably around 10 percent. Since the 1980s, the savings rate has fallen and now trends around 5 percent. Recessions generally cause the savings rate to spike, but the long-term trend in the United States is clear. The savings rate has basically halved.

This rate is lower than all but a handful of developed countries. Of course, adjustments need to be made for demographics and the degree of "safety net" that a government offers to replace the need for saving for emergencies such as unemployment or healthcare costs. However, even after considering both factors, it seems clear that the U.S. savings rate is insufficient for many to achieve a comfortable retirement.

Social Security presents an additional risk. In the United States, the amount Social Security expects to pay out exceeds the amount coming in. As the report of the Trustees of Medicare and Social Security report:

> Neither Medicare nor Social Security can sustain projected long-run program costs in full under currently scheduled financing, and legislative changes are necessary to avoid disruptive consequences for beneficiaries and taxpayers.[1]

The numbers of Social Security don't add up due to demographic trends. America has a rate of immigration that keeps its population, on

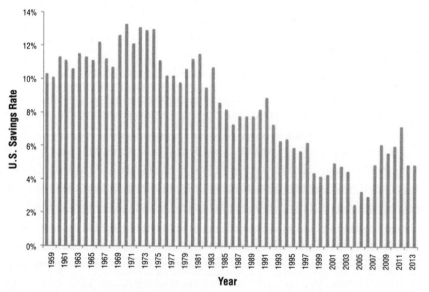

Figure 1.1   US Personal Savings Rate
Source: US. Bureau of Economic Analysis

average, younger than in many developed countries because immigrants tend to be younger than the average population. Despite this, the average age of the U.S. population is approximately 37,[2] and there will be increasingly more people in retirement than are working. That's a problem because the system is generally expected to balance what gets paid in (contributions from workers) with what gets paid out (payments to retirees). As retirees become a larger proportion of the population the balance breaks down. The Social Security problem is something that can be addressed with political will. However, doing so will likely mean a higher retirement age and potentially lower payments. As a result, reliance on individual savings is likely to increase.

Many people are ill prepared for retirement. Northwestern Mutual runs an annual study on the topic and finds that 42 percent of U.S. adults have not spoken to anyone about retirement, and that people are generally more comfortable talking about death or sex than retirement topics.[3] Often, those who have limited confidence in their retirement also describe themselves as having "debt problems," according to Employee Benefit Research Institute (ERBI) research.[4]

The Key Change in America's Retirement Planning Process

It used to be different. Previously, defined benefit plans avoided this problem; an employer took responsibility for retirement outcomes of their employers and the investment allocations to meet those needs.

Over time, the emphasis for most nongovernment employers has switched to providing contributions that employees can use to plan for their own retirement in 401(k) plans and similar tax-efficient vehicles. However, this apparently simple switch conceals a fundamental transfer of risk. Whereas previously employers bore the risk of their employees having a successful retirement, now employees carry the risk. The employer was once on the hook for providing a payout in retirement; now they no longer guarantee any payout in retirement. If the employee makes poor investment decisions or doesn't save enough, then their employer isn't going to step in and help when retirement comes. And, of course, most people are untrained in investment management.

An employer can be expected to bring in the expertise to understand investment allocations and cost minimization in retirement choices.

However, evidence suggests that employees can chase historic returns and use basic strategies such as investing 20 percent across each of five options that are present, even if some choices are very similar and some are not, or loading up on stock in their employer, since they are familiar with the company. These sorts of errors may seem trivial, but can translate into worse investment outcomes when compounded over decades. Other errors, such as significantly overpaying for investment advice or investing in dubious asset classes, can have far worse consequences.

Of course, advice is available, but while employers could find some of the best consultants available and spread that knowledge and benefits over thousands of workers, employees typically seek advice one on one, which is less efficient because it doesn't scale across a large group of people, and can cost as much as 2 percent of the employee's assets to get solid, if fairly generic, retirement advice. The problem of high-cost investments is discussed in detail in a later chapter, but unlike other goods and services, with investment advice you typically pay for the advice with the very savings you have, so high costs can make it hard to achieve your investment goals. This is unlike other purchases because with investment advice you are reducing your rate of return with the fees you pay in order to attempt to increase your rate of return—a direct contradiction. This is why keeping costs low matters.

How Financial Innovation Helps

Fortunately, just as the landscape for retirement support has changed, so innovation has enabled employees to get a better deal. Exchange-traded funds (ETFs) are a critical ingredient here. Unlike mutual funds, which have cost and tax inefficiencies, ETFs often provide the building blocks to assemble a robust portfolio at low cost. In conjunction, algorithmic advice can scale practically infinitely using technology. This provides portfolio management techniques that previously were the reserve of secretive quantitative teams to be publicly available. This means both the instruments and the techniques to ensure a successful retirement are now broadly available. The benefit here is not in lowering the costs of an existing service, but in expanding the reach of that service. Previously, even with relatively high fees, it simply wasn't economical for a financial advisor to serve a client with less than half a million in assets.

The percentage of assets to make it worth the advisor's time would eat into the client's investment returns and provide only a meager return for the advisor. This meant that prior to digital investment services, most of America was in the painful position of not necessarily wanting to manage their own investment portfolios, but often having to do so because there were few other viable choices open to them.

The Magic of a 15 Percent Savings Rate

However, we should remember that even the smartest techniques and lowest fees cannot solve the savings rate problem. Prospective returns can be improved but there is no magic wand. With a 6 percent rate of annual growth, you can double your money in 12 years, but if you save nothing, you'll still end up with nothing at the end. That's true however long you have to save and however well balanced a portfolio is on offer.

And, unfortunately, the savings challenge is getting harder, not easier. The global increase in life expectancy is a good thing, but it puts a lot more pressure on your retirement dollars that now have to last years longer than previously. Retirement actually is a relatively new phenomenon. Previously, people would quite literally work until they died. At the end of the Second World War, the average life expectancy of an American at birth was 65, meaning that many would have no retirement at all. Now, for those born in 2010, it is just over 78.[5] That is an increase of 13 years over two generations, and so retirement moves from being a short period to something most people can plan on experiencing for a decade or longer. The moves for an increased retirement age are unsurprising in the context of this stark improvement in life expectancy and quality of life for the elderly. Figure 1.2 shows U.S. life expectancy at age 65 over time, and the trend of increasing life expectancy is clear: this puts a greater burden on retirement savings as the retirement period lengthens.

Without proper planning, retirement may also be a luxury. This is an understandable outcome if Social Security diminishes in significance and savings rates remain at low levels. Increasingly, retirement is being delayed or potential retirees are continuing to work in old age. In the past two decades, the proportion of Americans expecting to retire after age 70 has more than doubled, from 9 percent to 26 percent, according

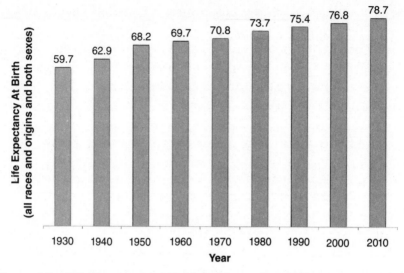

Figure 1.2 Life Expectancy in the United States since 1930

Source: Centers for Disease Control and Prevention

to EBRI data[6] from 1991 to 2015. Sometimes this is a lifestyle choice to remain active and engaged and avoid the abrupt lifestyle shift that retirement can represent. Now, 1 in 10 workers expects to carry on working into old age, and never retire, that figure has more than doubled recently, up from 4 percent in 1991. However, for many, delayed retirement is likely to be an economic necessity given the harsh reality of low savings rates.

Your savings rate makes a big difference to your retirement outcomes. Without Social Security payments, if you are able to earn 6 percent in real terms on your savings and spend 80 percent of your prior income in retirement and save consistently over 30 years, then a 5 percent savings rate, which is the around the current average savings rate in the United States can be expected to last around five years, which is shorter than most can expect to live in retirement by many years. And remember, many will live longer than the average life expectancy. A 10 percent savings rate may last around 16 years on similar assumptions. However, if you are able to save 15 percent or more from your income, then the same analytical framework suggests that you may be able to fund retirement from your savings indefinitely, since at a certain point the real income on the money you saved covers your retirement expenses. This is the ideal goal, since at this point you have sufficient financial security, even if you beat the odds and live much longer than actuarial tables would suggest.

Figure 1.3 shows life expectancy in the United States if you live to age 65. There's a good chance most people have 20 years of retirement, but longer periods of up to 40 years are quite possible. Jeanne Calment of France has the longest documented life span, living to be 122 years.

Of course, this is a relatively simple analysis, with Social Security or other strategies like selling your home and moving to a smaller one excluded. However, it does assume that you are able to live off 80 percent of your pre-retirement income.

One hidden benefit of a high savings rate, such as 15 percent, is that you are training yourself to live off less than your full income, which is helpful come retirement. Conversely, if you are using debt to finance expenses, then you are probably living off more than your income, which makes saving for retirement harder still. That's why a 15 percent savings rate is a good rule of thumb because you are not only building up a healthy nest egg, but you are living off 85 percent and that means your lifestyle is less expensive to fund in retirement than if you were spending 100 percent of your salary.

However, savings rates vary crucially with time to retirement. The preceding analysis assumes 30 years to retirement, for example, someone

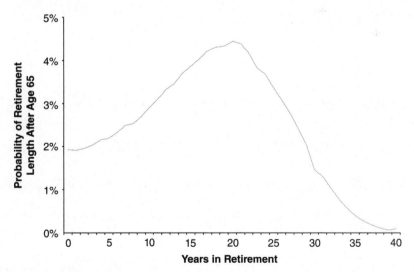

Figure 1.3 Years in Retirement

Source: National Vital Statistics System, 2007 U.S. Data for Both Sexes, FutureAdvisor Analysis

at age 34 looking to retire at 65. If you have more time, then your savings rate will be lower, but if you are older, then a similar savings rate won't meet your goal.

So America has a retirement problem. Savings rates are falling as life expectancy increases and the ability of Social Security to fully fund itself is in question. Fortunately, digital investment advice offers part of the solution in helping savers make robust investment decisions, but even the smartest investment systems cannot be effective if savings rates remain at very low levels.

KEY TAKEAWAYS

- America's savings rate is low relative to history.
- As life expectancy has increased, retirement has increased from a period of a few years after working to potentially many decades for some. Savings have not kept pace with this change.
- Saving 15 percent of your income over 30 years is ideal for a comfortable retirement.

Notes

1. Social Security and Medicare Board of Trustees, "A Summary of the 2014 Annual Reports," 2014.
2. Lindsay M. Howden and Julie A. Meyer, "U.S. Census Briefs, Age and Sex Composition: 2010," May 2011.
3. Northwestern Mutual, "2014 Planning and Progress Study."
4. Employee Benefit Research Institute and Greenwald and Associates, "Retirement Confidence Survey," 2015.
5. Elizabeth Arias, "National Vital Statistics Report," United States Life Tables, 2010.
6. Employee Benefit Research Institute and Greenwald and Associates, "Retirement Confidence Survey," 2015.

Chapter 2

The Risk of Not Investing in Stocks

"I'd like to live as a poor man with lots of money."

—Pablo Picasso

What if in Vegas there was a game where you could potentially double your money? Sure, you say, what are the odds? Oh, there's no major risk based on history, everyone who plays makes money, but some people make double or more. Okay, so what's the catch? Well, the catch is that the game takes 15 years from when you place your stake until you get your money back.

For many people that's a big hurdle. We are tuned into instant gratification. The credit industry means that many purchase things they can't even afford yet. McDonald's has served billions by serving a whole meal in under a minute or two. And get-rich-quick schemes of dubious quality are everywhere.

However, history suggests that if you have patience and persistence, you can make considerable money by having a prudent, long-term approach to investing. However, there is a catch, and it's in having a long-term focus and staying the course. The very reason the stock market is able to offer high returns—and the reason not everyone does it—is that it is considerably more risky over the short term.

The Short-Term Risks

Sometimes stocks are very risky—how does losing half your money in a year sound? How about seeing your investment fall in value for 5 of the months even in an average year? Well, that can be part and parcel of stock investing. In order to earn good returns, you need to stay the course, and sometimes that course can be very rocky. It might feel less like a path than a cliff. But if you put in your money, go away, and come back in 15 years, then you'll more than likely come out ahead if history is any guide.

Fortunately, most people have an investment goal that is well aligned with stock investing, namely, retirement. If you're in your 30s, then you have a few decades before you're planning to retire, and investing a significant proportion of your retirement savings in stocks is a good fit. Even if you're investing for a shorter period, such as to fund a child's college education or to put some money away for a few years to fund a deposit on a house, the stock market can still be useful component of the portfolio, but it will typically be a smaller portion as the time until you need the money shortens and the need to balance stock exposure with fixed-income instruments increases.

Additionally, you can construct a portfolio that may provide some insulation from the ups and downs of the stock market. Other assets can move up or decline less during bad periods for stocks, bringing more smoothness to your returns over time. This is the principle of diversification.

The Historical Perspective

Let's look at the evidence. Elroy Dimson and Paul Marsh have looked at stock markets from around the globe. They find that over the 1900–2014 period stock markets have delivered an actual average return after inflation of 5.2 percent. That compares with 1.9 percent for government bonds and 0.9 percent for government bills, again all numbers after inflation. Of course, these differences that may seem minor over the course of a year result in stark differences with compounding over time. A global equity portfolio would return more than seven times your initial investment over 40 years, and as I suggested at the start of this chapter, that rate of growth more than doubles your money after inflation in 15 years, whereas with bonds you'd more than double your money in 40 years, and with bills you'd earn almost a 50 percent incremental return. Also, the equity returns are robust across countries. Austria is at the low end with 0.6 percent return, and South Africa at the high end with a 7.4 percent return, but two-thirds of countries have average annual real equity returns of between 3 percent and 6 percent, consistent with the average level of growth seen across markets (see Figure 2.1).

Jeremy Siegel of Wharton has performed a similar analysis in the United States over two centuries and finds a real return on stocks of about 7 percent a year. Historically speaking, the United States has been at the higher end of returns relative to other markets, with only Australia and South Africa doing better within the Elroy, Dimson, and Marsh data set.

What is important about this data is not the absolute return that stocks deliver, though it is impressive, but that stocks consistently deliver

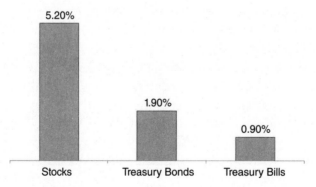

Figure 2.1   Historical Returns by Asset Class after Inflation, 1900–2014
Source: Elroy Dimson, Paul Marsh, and Mike Staunton, Triumph of the Optimists, Princeton University Press, 2002, and subsequent research

higher returns than other asset classes on a medium- or long-term view. That's what is relevant to the portfolio construction decision. Most strikingly, looking back from 1900 to 2014 in all of the countries where there is a full run of data, stocks outperform both bonds and bills. Clearly, there are periods of underperformance of stocks relative to bonds, often for a decade or more in some countries, but in the long-term view, stocks come out ahead.

The Logic

In addition to just looking at the historical numbers we can also consider logically why this is the case.

First, when an economy is growing, stocks are levered to that growth, and they receive the profit that is left after fixed costs are paid. So as an economy grows, returns to equity can grow disproportionately. This is not true of fixed-income investments, where returns over the bond's lifetime are capped by the coupon payment of the bond but could be less. While bonds offer a steady return, but with downside risk and no major upside, equities have more of a symmetrical risk profile in terms of potential upside and downside outcomes relative to bonds, which over the long term improves potential returns considerably. In addition, consider that although a stock can fall to zero—a loss of 100 percent—gains are not capped at 100 percent, since a stock can double or triple. The other benefit of stocks comes from pricing power.

When inflation increases, the real returns to fixed income decrease. You receive a 3 percent coupon whether inflation turns out to be 1 percent or 5 percent. However, for stocks, if inflation rises to 5 percent, companies have an opportunity to raise prices 5 percent. Clearly not all will and not all can due to the actions of customers, regulators, or competitors, but generally stocks have some defense against rising inflation, whereas bonds are more exposed to it. However, inflation is hardly plain sailing for stock investors, as we'll discuss in the next chapter.

So stocks are structurally set up to perform well. There is no cap on the upside of returns, and they have some moderate protection against inflation. The same cannot be said of fixed income, which is often more stable, but that stability comes at a cost of lower returns.

KEY TAKEAWAYS

- Stocks are volatile in the short term, but for a time period of 15 years or more, history suggests they are highly likely to deliver positive returns.
- Stocks have historically produced returns superior to those of fixed-income investments.
- Stocks have a generally favorable distribution of returns that can lead to superior long-term outcomes.

Chapter 3

The Enemies of a Stock Portfolio

"By a continuing process of inflation, government can confiscate, secretly and unobserved, an important part of the wealth of their citizens."

—John Maynard Keynes

One of the biggest enemies of your investment portfolio is rising inflation. Though stocks can fare better than many other investments during such periods, as the 1970s demonstrate, periods of inflation can still reduce stock returns. Inflation is when the cost of goods and services you buy rise in price. For example, if a can of Coke cost $1.50 last year and $1.65 this year, then that $0.15, or 10 percent, increase is inflation. The actual inflation metric that the government publishes is more complicated. This is because many things are purchased beyond Coke, so inflation calculations combine a diverse set of products and services according to their importance to get to one average inflation number. For example, food, which everyone needs, has a 13.8 percent weighting out of the 100 percent total, indoor plants and flowers, which are less commonly purchased, have a much lower 0.1 percent weighting. The price change of each component is monitored by the Bureau of Labor Statistics, which reports on U.S. inflation monthly. At the extremes over the past year, the price of televisions fell 15 percent, but the price of certain footwear rose 8.3 percent. Most products stay relatively close to the average inflation rate, which two-thirds of the time in U.S. history has fallen in a 1 percent to 4 percent range. However, the other third of the time matters; inflation in the United States has been as high as 15 percent in recent history.

Why Inflation Matters

Inflation matters for you as an investor because your investments are priced in dollars. If your Apple stock is trading at $100 in your retirement fund, and you plan to drink a lot of Coke in retirement, then your Apple stock is less valuable if the price of a Coke is $1.65 rather than $1.50. This is true even if the price of Apple stock is unchanged. You can now buy six fewer cans of Coke with your Apple investment than you previously could. That's why inflation hurts you as an investor—your investment dollars are worth less when you ultimately come to spend them if prices rise over time.

This problem is true for many fundamental types of investment. Bonds are hurt by inflation because their payments are fixed in dollar terms. Stocks may ultimately fare somewhat better because companies may be able to raise prices to compensate for inflation, but, for example, rising inflation in the mid-1970s hitting double digits was one of the factors that caused the Standard & Poor's (S&P) 500 to almost halve over three years. As stock investors, you need to pay attention to inflation. Given that the fundamental constituents of most portfolios are stocks and bonds, we have a problem here. Stocks and bonds generally pair well together to manage many economic risks, but unfortunately rising inflation is not one of those risks. It hurts both stocks and bonds.

Treasury Inflation-Protected Securities (TIPS)

Fortunately, the U.S. government has an investment that helps manage inflation. It's a unique and sometimes misunderstood asset class called Treasury inflation-protected securities (TIPS). TIPS have only existed since 1997, so while stocks and bonds have historical data going back centuries, TIPS are relatively new. TIPS are designed to compensate you for inflation. When the Consumer Price Index for Urban Consumers (CPI-U), a broadly used measure of inflation, rises unexpectedly, the value of your investment goes up and not down as other asset classes are likely to. This makes TIPS an unusually useful asset class for your portfolio.

However, there are also a few myths to dispel about TIPS. First, TIPS can have a negative yield. This can be a concern, but this yield is before the inflation adjustment (which cannot be known in advance), so if the yield is −0.25 percent but inflation is 2 percent, then TIPS would return +1.75 percent assuming that other factors didn't impact the price such as changes in market sentiment. This is largely a reflection of low yields on fixed-income assets, but it is important to remember that you are purchasing TIPS for protection against unexpected inflation, and in that case it's probable that, due to their design, the return from TIPS would increase.

Second, a correlation matrix can be a useful tool to design a portfolio by looking at how investments have done relative to each other in the past. This is generally a valid technique, but given the short life span of TIPS, it is less useful because the scenario where TIPS are most useful has not played out in the United States in the past 14 years while TIPS have existed. CPI-U inflation has generally stayed in a relatively narrow range. Therefore, we haven't seen the scenario where TIPS fare best; however, the experience of the United States in the 1970s certainly shows that rising inflation is a real scenario, as you can see in Figure 3.1.

Buying TIPS directly can be cumbersome, so using exchange-traded funds (ETFs) to access TIPs in a low-cost and highly liquid form makes sense. For example, Vanguard has a low-cost short-term TIPS fund (VTIP), and iShares has a similar short-term TIPS fund (STIP). Shorter-term TIPS funds can make sense because historically in the United States inflation spikes have been short term in nature and these funds typically

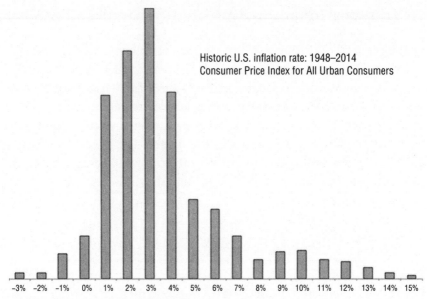

Historic U.S. inflation rate: 1948–2014
Consumer Price Index for All Urban Consumers

Figure 3.1   Historical U.S. Inflation Chart
Source: U.S. Bureau of Labor Statistics

have lower volatility with their lower duration. Schwab U.S. TIPS ETF (SCHP) is another reasonable option, but the duration is slightly longer and the iShares TIPS Bond ETF (TIP) is slightly expensive relative to others in terms of expense ratio at the time of writing.

Remember that TIPS can be a relatively tax-inefficient investment. Income and capital gains are taxed at the same rate as ordinary income. This means it can be best to hold them in a tax-efficient savings vehicle like an individual retirement account (IRA) or 401(k).

Overall, I believe well-constructed portfolios consider all potential adverse scenarios to preserve capital. Based on U.S. history, rising inflation is possible and would impact stocks and bonds were it to occur. TIPS can provide valuable protection for that scenario.

Asset Confiscation

The second major risk to stocks is simply confiscation of assets. This is rare but has occurred in both Russia and in China in the twentieth century. When a country decides to move away from being a market-based economy, then private assets (including stocks) can be confiscated. Of course, both China and Russia have reversed course subsequently allowing some degree of capitalism within their economies, but of course this is little comfort to those investing in stocks in these countries at the time of confiscation. They never received them back. Though the risk here appears small in the context of history, the impact can be devastating and it demonstrates the benefit of country diversification to help manage this risk, which we'll discuss in Chapter 8.

Recession

The final major risk to stock investors is recession. Normally, economies grow over time, so each year more goods and services are produced. However, a recession occurs when the economy goes into reverse and shrinks. This is normally temporary, but given that stocks are sensitive to growth rates recessions normally cause stock declines. Table 3.1 shows the characteristics of some of the four largest recessions in terms of GDP decline for the United States in the twentieth century. Three of these were accompanied by major stock declines. As you can see from the final column, recessions are also generally accompanied by strong increases in the stock market once they end.

Recessions are an inseparable part of stock market investing. International diversification can help diversify across economies, but ultimately trying to time the markets around recessions is extremely challenging and can lead to worse outcomes. As Paul Samuelson wrote, "Wall Street indexes predicted nine out of the last five recessions."

Table 3.1 Major U.S. Recessions

Name	Start	GDP Decline	Peak Unemployment	S&P 500 Max. Decline	S&P 500 One-Year Rebound Off Lows
Great Depression	1929	−27%	25%	−86%	118%
Postwar Recession	1945	−13%	5%	Stock market rose	n/a
1937 Recession	1937	−18%	19%	−45%	10%
Great Recession	2007	−4%	10%	−57%	52%

Source: FutureAdvisor analysis

KEY TAKEAWAYS

- Rising inflation can hurt a stock portfolio, even though other assets may fare even worse.
- The U.S. experience in the 1970s demonstrates this risk.
- Inclusion of TIPS in a portfolio has the potential to help manage this risk.
- Asset confiscation is a small but strongly negative risk for a stock portfolio.
- Recessions generally lead to stock market declines, but also often see markets rise strongly as they end.

Chapter 4

The Value of Time for Investors

"I never attempt to make money on the stock market. I buy on the assumption that they could close the market the next day and not reopen it for five years."

—Warren Buffett

Why Long-Term Stock Investing Is Less Risky than It May Seem

A digital investment process must, at its core, be built on robust market assumptions. One key tenet is the belief in equities as an attractive asset class for the long term, often with surprisingly low long-term risk, if history is any guide when stocks are held for decades.

Of course, one of the challenges in investing is that in the short term the market can appear very risky. Over the course of a single day, month, or year an investor can lose roughly 5 percent, 10 percent, or 40 percent of their money, respectively. And that's true even if you're tracking a low-cost diversified index—if you're betting on a few single stocks, you could fare even worse. Just ask investors who loaded up on tech stocks in 2000 or certain banks in 2008. Of course, asset class diversification, as I discuss elsewhere, can offset these losses to a degree, depending on what motivates the market decline.

However, the fact remains that in the short-term market outcomes can appear downright scary. It's easy to underestimate the problem short-term declines present on paper, because if you see them on a stock chart, you view the whole picture in retrospect—both the decline and, typically, the subsequent recovery. You have the advantage of seeing the future. However, living through them, you experience the decline and lots of red in your portfolio before you see any recovery. The chart looks like a black diamond ski slope rather than a "V" shape that typically oc-curs as the markets rebound over time.

The Long-Term Picture

The good news is that the picture over the long term is quite different, and lower risk, on any day. Your odds are about 50/50 of stocks going up based on history, but over 10 years, you'll see stocks rise over 9 times out of 10, and as your time horizon lengthens, those odds generally improve further.

Let's stop for a second here. This is a critical point. But like most impor-tant points, it's not easy to understand. Often, when we see something that's risky in the short term, we expect the long term will follow a similar pattern. To use a coin toss example, you can toss a coin repeatedly and the odds aren't going to change one bit. It's a 50 percent chance of heads on toss 1 or toss 100.

Historically, the markets haven't been like that. If you look at the short term, the market is an unpredictable roller coaster, but in the long term, say a decade or more, the markets can be a fairly stable wealth-generating machine. Let's look at the history in the United States. Going back to 1881 looking at every 15-year period for the Standard & Poor's (S&P) 500, the market has made money for investors on a real basis after taking account of dividends. The reason is that even though the daily market movement is almost a coin toss, the odds are actually very slightly in your favor on any given day. Over the course of a day, a week, or a month, this historical effect of having a slightly better than even chance of making money is drowned out by the very large volatility in stock movements. Consider that the average return to stocks is around 7 percent, but in a single year major stock indices have risen or fallen over 50 percent. It's clear that the considerable volatility in stocks drowns out their steady upward march in the short term. Nonetheless, over time, the slight tendency of stocks to deliver a positive return on an average day becomes a powerful effect when observed over many years, even years that can contain pretty worrying declines.

Figure 4.1 illustrates this point. It shows the historical distribution of U.S. stock market returns from 1928 to 2014. Remember that with investing, you typically have two goals. The first is to achieve the maximum returns you can. In the case of Figure 4.1, that means to see returns as far to the right as possible. The second is to minimize risk, and again in the case of Figure 4.1, ideally to see a bunching of returns with high probability. It shows the distribution of stock market returns over historical 1-, 3-, and 10-year periods.

As you can see, within a single year, the range of outcomes for the stock market is broad. Over a single year, historical returns have ranged between −50 percent and +60 percent you can see a positive skew in

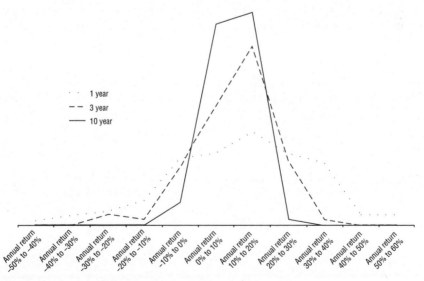

Figure 4.1 U.S. Market Returns over Time

returns, in that returns are likely to be more positive than negative. Then on a 3-year view, returns become more grouped in positive territory and the chance of an extreme loss declines. Then on a 10-year view, market returns all fall within the −10 percent to +30 percent range.

There are some important caveats here. The biggest one is that 10 years is a long time and you have to stay in the market through what feels like the worst of times. In fact, of course, 10 years is too long if you know you're going to need money within 5 years. If that's the case, then the stock market is a much riskier place to be.

So if you're investing for retirement and in your 40s or younger, then the stock market is likely a sound investment option. You won't need the money for 20 years at the very earliest and history shows that over that time period the stock markets generally rise and generally fare better than other mainstream asset classes in terms of return. This is why equities form the bulk of a traditional portfolio, since if your time horizon is long enough, then history shows the prospect of a reasonable return with limited chance of a bad outcome.

How Bonds Can Help

However, adding bonds to a portfolio can help reduce risk further. Figure 4.2 compares one-year returns for bonds and stocks. Whereas stocks require a longer-term holding period to achieve reasonable confidence

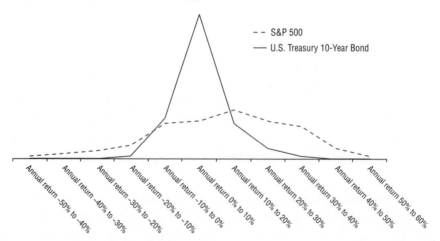

Figure 4.2   Stocks vs. Bonds over Time

in a good outcome, for bonds even shorter holding periods can yield good results.

Bonds matter because in order to experience the long-term growth that equities enjoy, you must stay invested in equities, and that's harder than it sounds when you are enduring market declines. The value of bonds comes in three forms. First, as Figure 4.2 shows, they are more stable than equities, so a portfolio with bonds is more stable than a portfolio with just equities. Second, bonds actually go one better than being merely stable; they can perform relatively well when equities are weak.

Going back to 1928, the U.S. 10-year bond has risen 88 percent of the time when the S&P 500 has fallen for the year, and 79 percent of the time in years when stocks were up, so bonds are not merely stable but can actually actively balance a stock portfolio because they tend to perform even better when stocks decline. Third, with a portfolio that employs rebalancing, bonds can be helpful in market declines, because rebalancing creates an opportunity to sell bonds, which have often risen in value, at a time when equities have fallen in value. This can be helpful because having money to buy stocks at times when they may be relatively inexpensive can help returns, and bonds can offer this benefit.

Aside from the time changing the fundamental odds of coming out ahead with stocks, time also puts the power of compounding on your side. Albert Einstein called compound interest "the eighth wonder of the world." The value of compounding is that as your money grows and you reinvest it, your wealth increases faster because your earnings from earlier years start generating additional returns as well. As Table 4.1 shows, the results of this can be impressive. For example, at a 4 percent annual rate of return, your money can double in 18 years, and at 8 percent your money can double in a decade. This also implies a robust strategy for building wealth, often extremely aggressive investment strategies that promise 20 percent returns or more can fail, but a slower and steadier strategy that enjoys returns in the high single digits can double your wealth faster than you might expect. However, again, the key weapon here is not astronomical annual returns but the passage of time. By implementing your investment strategy as soon as you can, you give your money the maximum amount of time to work for you and thereby improve your prospects of building wealth. This is one reason that it's helpful to reinvest dividends and interest back into your portfolio. At FutureAdvisor we find that this income not only boosts your returns when reinvested due to compounding, but also can provide a source of funds for rebalancing a portfolio without requiring the sale of existing assets, regular cash contributions into a portfolio can achieve the same result. Table 4.1 shows that returns, which have been achieved by stocks historically, can cause the value of your investment to double in under 20 years.

The final point to make about time in investing is that value of having a strategy that you can stick to for the long term. It's easy to maintain a strategy in good markets and even edge up your belief in the amount of risk that you can stomach. However, in bad markets, you might find that you can tolerate less risk than you thought. Just as 93 percent of people believe that they have better driving skills than average,[1] so investors tend to believe they have superior ability to endure a bad market than average. This is called *illusory superiority,* and it can hurt your investment returns. It's important to have a strategy than you can maintain for the long term in order to grow your wealth and not underestimate your ability to manage risk. As the numbers above show, sometimes taking slightly less risk and forgoing some return may be worth it if it means you can maintain your investment strategy for the coming decades. A single-digit return, if sustained, can help your portfolio grow significantly for the long term.

Table 4.1   Years It Takes Your Money to Double

Annual Rate of Return	Number of Years for Portfolio to Double
4%	18
5%	15
6%	12
7%	11
8%	10

Source: FutureAdvisor analysis

KEY TAKEAWAYS

- Stocks are risky in the short term, but for a long-term investor investing for 10 years or more, the risks of loss have been much lower.
- Bonds can further improve this risk profile by bringing stability to a portfolio and providing funds to purchase stocks when they fall in value.
- Compounding can also help the long-term investor to achieve impressive results based on high-single-digit returns when funds are invested for a decade or more.
- However, the long-term investment approach works only if you can stick with your strategy in bad markets. Many investors miss out on returns by changing strategy, such as moving to cash, in bad market conditions.

Note

1. Ola Svenson, "Are We All Less Risky and More Skillful than Our Fellow Drivers?" *Acta Psychologica* 47(2) (February 1981): 143–148.

Chapter 5

Core Assets of a Robust Portfolio

"Don't look for the needle in the haystack. Just buy the hay-stack!"

—John C. Bogle

T his chapter assesses the asset classes that do and don't merit a place in a well-diversified portfolio.

Asset Classes We Include

U.S. Equities

The case for long-term investment in U.S. equities is compelling. In a sense, over the past two centuries, the United States has gone from an emerging market to an economic superpower—an emerging market that has truly emerged. That accounts for the 6.5-7 percent annual

average returns that Siegel documents.[1] This finding is generally robust across time periods of a decade or more showing equities to be
the most desirable asset class among highly liquid, publicly available
investments.

Within U.S. equities, broad market indices appear an attractive way
to invest. Broader indices typically have fewer rules associated with
inclusion/exclusion and so turnover is lower. Diversification can be
higher, though equal weighting may improve diversification and returns,
but at the time of writing the cost of implementation is likely to offset the benefit, in our view, given the 0.5 percent difference in fees
between the two approaches and when many small-cap funds are available at much lower cost, allowing a similar, if not identical, pivot to equal
weighting.

U.S. Value and Small Cap

U.S. value stocks have typically outperformed the broader U.S. stock
benchmark. This effect increases with stock cheapness as assessed on
a price-to-earnings (P/E), yield, or price-to-book (P/B) basis.[2] Once
again, there is a trade-off between the expensive cost of certain value
tilts versus a low-cost approach. Generally, I would expect better returns
from the lower-cost value funds, even though their tilts may not be as
extreme as I would optimally like in the absence of varying fees across
approaches.

Some argue that the outperformance of value is an anomaly due to
statistical data mining. I reject this because value performs well out of
sample and across most geographies. I also believe that developments in
behavioral finance are instructive in showing that investors are not perfectly rational in their behavior[3] and arbitrage is never costless,[4] so holding value stocks is not necessarily easy or intuitive when these stocks
can have poor track records and reputations. Also note that value stocks
can be riskier over the short term, but given that we are managing
portfolios for the long term, I believe we can overcome this constraint,
whereas many investors who are investing over shorter time horizons
cannot.

Small cap has a similar track record in offering strong historic
returns. I discuss these tilts in more detail in Chapter 14.

Developed Market Equities

Evidence on home bias in investing is persuasive and the prospects are good for achieving a smoother return with international diversification. It is generally the case that, at the time of writing, valuations in other developed markets, especially in Europe, are more attractive than the United States, and this may support slightly higher long-term returns in developed markets outside the United States in the coming years, since it is likely that growth and inflation follow relatively similar profiles globally for developed markets. In drawdown scenarios, I see developed markets performing similarly to the United States.

Emerging Markets

There is potentially opportunity in emerging markets for the long-term investor. Valuations are at a 20 percent to 30 percent discount to developed markets as of 2015. There is potential for that gap to narrow over time, supported by demographic trends and economic development. However, even if that discount persists, it may offer the potential for slightly higher returns from emerging-market stocks based on valuation alone. Emerging markets make up a much smaller proportion of the global market capitalization of stocks than of their gross domestic product (GDP), which may also be an indication of value. Of course, emerging-market stocks can have higher volatility and greater falls in value in the short term, but the prospect of higher returns more than offsets these risks for a long-term investor.

Real Estate Investment Trusts (REITs)

REITs have interesting properties in a portfolio context. Returns are broadly similar to the U.S. market, but given that their valuation is supported by real assets, they can perform relatively well at times of rising inflation. This is important because it enables REITs to offer some inflation hedge without a significant return cost.

International Real Estate

I believe that international real estate can smooth returns while providing similar inflation hedging and generally attractive returns.

U.S. Fixed Income

As you may remember from earlier chapters, equities generally outperform bonds over any long time period of a decade or more. However,
fixed income still has real benefits. U.S. fixed income is the most consistent and robust hedge to U.S. equities. The correlations between other
asset classes can change over time, but the relationship between U.S.
equities and debt is about as robust as asset class correlations get. Most
equity instruments, whether in different sectors or asset classes, will generally move down together in a bad market. The degree and timing of
the move may be slightly different, but in a bad market it is challenging
to hedge an equity position with other equities.

In addition, asset classes such as commodities are better considered uncorrelated with equities. That means that they basically move
independently. In a portfolio context, this is good; holding a large number of assets that move independently will serve you well. However, you
cannot be sure that commodities will be moving up when equities are
moving down. Historically, in many cases, they have not. Fortunately,
most of the time in an equity market decline there is a "flight to quality,"
and investors have a tendency to move money from equities into bonds,
as occurred in both 2000 and in 2008 in the United States.

Fixed income has also offered a reasonable long-term return in
addition to the diversification benefit. As such, fixed income can be considered insurance to your equity portfolio, but unlike more complex
option-based strategies—which can be challenging to implement and
typically result in a loss if the market moves in the other direction and
can fall in value over time—fixed income provides an income stream in
addition to potentially helping you in a bad equity market. It's something like insurance where you are paid to hold it.

Clearly, there is an opportunity cost because over the longer term,
fixed-income returns will likely lag equities, but by using a glidepath,
which reduces your stock exposure as retirement nears (see Figure 5.1),
you can tailor the fixed-income exposure in your portfolio to make sure
that you aren't taking more risk than your time horizon can tolerate.
That's important because if you take on more risk than you can handle
and move to cash, or adopt a similarly conservative strategy in a bad
market, that can hurt your long-term returns.

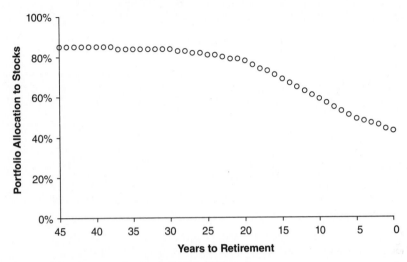

Figure 5.1 An Example Stock/Bond Glidepath

Source: FutureAdvisor

International Fixed Income

As in equity, we believe that international diversification can smooth returns for fixed income. In the United States, returns to fixed income are related to the action of the Federal Reserve in setting interest rates, which in turn is related to the prospects for the U.S. economy. To the extent that different countries are at different points in the business cycle, international diversification can smooth returns. International fixed income can also introduce some currency exposure into portfolios, which can also be beneficial in helping to smooth returns.

Treasury Inflation-Protected Securities (TIPS)

Based on the experience of Europe, where inflation-protected securities are a broader proportion of the fixed-income market, I believe TIPS have the opportunity for growth and are well designed for capital preservation, especially at times of rising inflation, as discussed in Chapter 3. TIPS are generally similar to other fixed-income products, but the return on them is directly linked to the rate of inflation rather than a predetermined coupon payment each year. As a result, if inflation rises unexpectedly, then TIPS holders will receive a higher payment, but traditional bonds may see a decline in value. The reverse is true, too; where inflation is lower than expected, TIPS may underperform traditional fixed income, assuming no other factors are at play. I generally recommend short-duration holdings of TIPS because historically periods of rising inflation have been short lived. Robust protection against rising inflation is difficult to find in a low-cost portfolio context, so, at FutureAdvisor, we look to TIPS to fill that role, with real estate taking a supporting position.

Individual Asset Classes We Exclude

Generally, following theoretical logic, including more diversified assets within a portfolio can help the risk-return trade-off in a portfolio, since every asset is likely to bring some diversification to the portfolio at the margin. However, though that works in theory, in practice the presence of high fees, selection biases, and tax inefficiencies makes many assets ultimately unattractive. Of course, this is something to monitor on an ongoing basis. Reduced fees, changes in the tax code, or innovations in the structuring of new exchange-traded funds (ETFs) could change our position on these topics on a multiyear view, so I continue to monitor developments with interest for several of these asset classes. ETFs have been around for only a few decades, and we've seen a lot of innovation over that period, so it's possible that innovation brings additional assets in a transparent, liquid, and low-cost form that makes sense to include in portfolios.

The Risks of Illiquid Investments in a Portfolio

I recommend excluding various investments from a portfolio for a single reason—illiquidity. This means these investments can be hard to buy and sell, often at the times you most want to buy and sell them. Illiquid investments pose a problem for investors because they cannot be easily rebalanced. Illiquid investments by definition are ones that you cannot trade as often as you wish, and there may in fact be penalties in terms of a lower realized price for trading assets that are illiquid. In a portfolio context, this is a problem; for example, if equities fall in value and the rebalancing rules of the portfolio dictate purchasing more equities, then something must be sold to raise the funds for the purchase. This may not be possible with illiquid assets because they cannot be sold quickly enough to raise cash for the purchase or at reasonable values. Furthermore, if the illiquid asset itself outperforms the broader market, portfolio rules would dictate a sale, and again this may not be possible. Therefore, illiquid assets not only pose direct risks to the portfolio due to their illiquidity but can also interfere with and potentially counteract some of the benefits of rebalancing policies, leading to increased portfolio risk.

Peer-to-Peer Lending

Peer-to-peer lending may be an attractive asset class for the long term from a return standpoint. However, currently high fees, potential illiquidity, legal constraints on investors from certain states, and tax inefficiency prevent usage of the asset class today. Certainly, consumer lending has been a great business for banks and credit card companies historically, and returns appear attractive over both the short run of data that is available and longer-term economic data. Greater openness of new platforms such as Lending Club and Prosper in the United States and many other firms internationally offer opportunity. Of course, they may also change the fundamental structure of the industry with lax loan standards or by depressing returns through more transparent and open competition. I continue to monitor the asset class as a medium-term opportunity and am generally optimistic. One fundamental issue for the type of portfolios we construct is the relatively low liquidity in peer-to-peer lending currently. Though you can purchase a diverse range of fixed-income investments that mature in under five years, there it limited ability to sell down your position within the course of a day without seeing significant impairment of the value to help complete a sale. Whereas ETFs can be bought and sold with minimal friction, the same cannot be said of peer-to-peer lending at the present time.

Venture Capital

The primary challenge with return capital is that although returns are attractive and somewhat diversified from public equity, returns are skewed to top-performing funds. I welcome innovation from the JOBS Act, among other factors, in making the asset class more broadly accessible. It is a concern that the current vehicles for investment suffer from adverse selection in that the best deals are likely not part of their portfolios, and this will hurt their returns. To a greater extent than other asset classes, returns to the asset class vary strongly by firm. The top firms get their pick of deals and often earn high returns as a result. However, the average firm tends to earn a much lower return. Liquidity and fee structures are also material concerns with this asset class.

Private Equity

Similar concerns to venture capital apply here, although the correlation with public equity performance is greater. Also, there seems to be a general belief that private equity offers the prospect of greater returns, but studies of performance have shown returns on private equity to be very similar to those of public equity.[5] In addition, unlike the public equity markets, a single ETF can hold thousands of individual investments. Attaining the same level of robust diversification and basic monitoring/reporting standards among a range of public equity investments is far more challenging. Fundamentally, private equity is not much different than public equity and with much greater frictions associated with investment, and thus we exclude it from FutureAdvisor portfolios. Finally, there is some evidence that certain top-tier private equity funds can perform better than average,[6] but these funds are typically not broadly accessible to the public.

Cash (as an Investment Class)

We may hold a small amount of cash in cases based on optimization of waiting until enough cash is on hand to merit investment. However, I believe historical data are compelling that the value of cash is eroded by inflation over time and returns are dominated by many other assets. Cash does have the property of stability in adverse markets, but history has shown that fixed income instruments offer an generally superior risk-return trade-off within a portfolio. When investing for the short term of approximately five years or less, I believe cash can have a role to play given its relative stability and liquidity.

High-Yield Debt

High-yield debt offers slightly lower returns than equities but greater risk than most fixed-income instruments. I believe high yield is dominated in a portfolio context by a combination of equity and debt. In addition, high yield is a relatively high-cost asset class within ETFs with a cost of 40 to 65 basis points (bps) for major funds (or 5 to 10 times comparable equity and debt ETFs), which I believe dampens returns when a combination of other equity and fixed-income ETFs can achieve a similar outcome at lower cost.

Commodities

Commodities do not offer an intrinsic return to investors in the manner of a dividend or buyback from a stock or a coupon from a bond. As such, they are hard to value with any precision, and long-term performance appears relatively weak depending on the time period. They do offer some diversification benefit, but I believe real estate and TIPS offer superior characteristics here. Real estate generally enjoys superior long-term returns and offers some inflation hedge. TIPS offer a more consistent inflation hedge by virtue of how they are constructed. In addition, a well-diversified commodity ETF (metals, timber, agricultural commodities, and energy) currently has a relatively high expense ratio, which can significantly erode returns. Lower-cost commodity funds focus on a subset of commodities, which presents additional risk and greater exposure to specific supply-and-demand dynamics than inflation risk management.

There are also some ETFs that create commodity exposure through holding stocks that process and produce commodities such as gold miners or oil companies. This certainly reduces the implementation cost but doesn't meet the goal of diversification because these stocks will already be present in diversified benchmarks and will, despite some exposure to commodity values, trade in a similar way to the broader stock market during most market scenarios because the change in the discounting of future earnings and other factors will have the potential to have more impact on the price of these stocks than the impact of commodity pricing. Also, certain commodities can be tax inefficient; for example, gold and silver funds can be cheaper ways to obtain commodity exposure within the ETF universe. However, the IRS can tax these as "collectibles," which typically incur a higher tax rate than other investments and can offset the benefits through introducing higher costs.

Hedge Funds

While in theory hedge funds offer the promise of attractive returns and limited equity correlation, in practice I see generally weak returns and high correlation with equities. Generally, enthusiasm for this asset class appears to be waning given weak historical returns and extremely high fees in some cases. Hedge funds also typically involve an active approach, where I believe the odds are against success. Fees are again relatively high here, in the 70 to 100 bps range, which creates a significant headwind for returns. As with private equity or venture capital, there are also adverse selection risks. Those funds that are freely available to a broad set of investors are not necessarily the best funds, as those can attract investors without reaching out to the public at large. As with the category of other portfolio tilts, it's possible that something emerges within this space with attractive risk-return properties and low cost, but I'm not seeing it currently based on historical analysis. Again, there are strategies here that are academically robust, but fees and taxes associated with implementation tend to more than offset the benefits.

Leveraged ETFs

Leveraged ETFs are useful to some traders on an extremely short-term basis, but over any extended holding period I expect them to decline in value almost by design and do not hold them. For a short-term and very active portfolio manager, they may prove to be useful trading instruments, but given our more passive buy-and-hold approach, I view these as unsuitable.

KEY TAKEAWAYS

- A diverse set of assets should be included in a portfolio to balance risks over time.
- REITs and TIPS can hedge rising inflation.
- Fixed income can hedge weak economic growth.
- Including illiquid assets can be problematic for effective rebalancing and hurt returns as a result.

Notes

1. Jeremy J. Siegel, *The Future For Investors*. New York, NY: Random House Inc., 2005.
2. Eugene F. Fama and Kenneth R. French, "The Cross-Section of Expected Stock Returns." *Journal of Finance* 47(2) (June 1992): 427–465.
3. Nicholas Barberis and Richard Thaler, "A Survey of Behavioral Finance." In *Handbook of the Economics of Finance,* vol. 1, Part 2, edited by G. M. Constantinides, M. Harris, and R. M. Stulz, 1053–1128. Amsterdam, Netherlands, 2003.
4. Andrei Shleifer and Robert W. Vishny, "The Limits of Arbitrage." *The Journal of Finance* 52(1) (March 1997): 35–55.
5. Tobias J. Moskowitz and Annette Vissing-Jorgensen, "The Returns to Entrepreneurial Investment: A Private Equity Premium Puzzle?" NBER Working Paper No. 8876, 2002.
6. Steven Kaplan and Antointette Schoar, "Private Equity Performance: Returns, Persistence, and Capital Flows." *The Journal of Finance* 60(4) (2005): 1791–1823.

Chapter 6

Dynamic Asset Selection

Determining the Lowest-Cost Option for Each Portfolio

"I do not fear computers. I fear the lack of them."

—Isaac Asimov

Garry Kasparov was a chess prodigy. He grew up in what is now Azerbaijan on the Caspian Sea, and won the Soviet junior chess championships at age 13. At the age of just 22, Garry Kasparov became the youngest chess world champion. He held that title for all but three months of almost two decades. With a tremendous capacity for study and an aggressive opening style, he is regarded as one of the greatest chess players of all time.

However, even as great a player as Kasparov made mistakes and lost games, with key matches sometimes hinging on a single game or draw. From a historical perspective, what is more significant about Kasparov's time as champion is the rise of a computer's ability to play chess at the highest level and win.

At the start of his tenure as world chess champion, computers were little match for Kasparov. He could play 32 chess computers simultaneously, as he did in Hamburg in 1985, and beat all of them. Computers couldn't pose a challenge to him when he started. But things changed. A decade later, a chess computer, Deep Thought, was estimated to have attained grand master status in its playing ability. However, Kasparov beat grand masters all the time, and Deep Thought was no exception.

In 1996, the watershed happened and Kasparov lost a game, to IBM's computer Deep Blue, but still won the match 4–2. Just over a year later, on May 11, 1997, Kasparov lost an entire six-game match to Deep Blue outright. Kasparov wasn't happy. In particular, he resented being denied access to Deep Blue's recent games to study before the match, as was his style. The writing was on the wall, though; by the mid-2000s, computers were winning tournaments against an entire slate of human grand masters outright, and then the humans started getting various advantages and still lost. By then, it was over. By 2009, software running on a mobile phone reached grand master level and after a brief period of hype, media attention, and million-dollar prize money, computer versus human chess games no longer get any attention.

Humans haven't changed. Computers have. Grand masters have always made mistakes, but computers don't make errors in the same way, and as the processing power of computers has increased, they can look further and further ahead, evaluating more and more potential outcomes. Deep Blue was capable of exploring 200 million chess positions in a single second. What beat Kasparov was brute force in a game of the intellectual elite.

Similar processes can perform fund selection across tens of thousands of client portfolios extremely well. After losing to Deep Blue, Kasparov said the computer was "only intelligent in the way your programmable alarm clock is intelligent. Not that losing to a $10 million alarm clock makes me feel any better."

In perhaps trying to demean the computer's accomplishment, Kasparov also reinforces the incredible reliability of computers with the alarm clock analogy. It's a task like tax loss harvesting, where vigilant and rules-based monitoring can provide incremental performance. There are many factors that impact trading costs, and an algorithm has the potential to consider all of them relative to the benefit a trade provides. Just as in chess, humans, even the best humans will make occasional mistakes. Sometimes those mistakes will cost a match, other times they won't be as significant, but computing power, especially now with almost infinitely scalable cloud infrastructure behind it, can perform complex portfolio maintenance decisions and avoid mistakes.

One of the fundamental components is the expense ratio of the fund itself. It may seem obvious that this is the value to minimize, but actually in the case of smaller clients or less liquid markets other factors may dominate, especially when you have a prescreened list of funds that are already extremely low cost.

Consider the following example. Client A has $20,000 allocation to U.S. equities, Client B has a smaller portfolio and resulting U.S. equities is just $2,000 of the portfolio.

Now assume two available funds, Fund X has 0.15 percent expense ratio, 0.1 percent bid-ask spread and trades commission free with the brokerage where Client A and Client B have as their custodian. Fund Y has a 0.05 percent expense ratio, a 0.1 percent bid-ask spread and the round-trip commission is $10.

So for Client A, over a three-year holding period, the cost of X is $110, whereas Y is $60. Hence, assuming the funds are similar in terms of construction, tracking error, and other factors, Fund Y is the better choice for Client A. His larger position size means that the expense ratio dominates the other factors. Now, conversely, for Client B, Fund X is the better choice, costing $20 rather than $22 for Fund Y over three years. Given the smaller position size, the need to trade commission free becomes the dominant factor.

An important overlay on the trading process also relates to tax loss harvesting. Wash sales, which involve trading a stock within 30 days of prior trade, can eliminate tax loss harvesting benefits, so the algorithm is able to know that and avoid funds that might create wash sales. This is why it's important for any asset manager to have an overview of all household accounts, so that a wash sale is not inadvertently created by a trade in another account. If an advisor is just managing one of your accounts, then trades elsewhere in your account—especially where popular funds are being used—have the potential to create a wash sale.

Another factor that algorithms should consider is dynamic allocation with respect to portfolio size. This is another form of optimization with respect to trading costs. Some asset classes are essential for portfolio construction for a portfolio of any size. For example, an appropriate bond/equity split is an integral driver of the risk and return of a portfolio, and asset classes that fill an important diversification role, from REITs to TIPS to international exposure, should also be represented or the portfolio cost can be significant.

However, in certain cases, adding every asset class to a small portfolio creates a situation where the cost exceeds the benefit. For example, if allocation to U.S. small cap would be very small and expensive to implement on a commission basis, then the algorithm is able to trade off the diversification score (as a measure of the value of inclusion) against the cost of implementation. This is the case because an asset class such as U.S. small cap may provide some incremental return, but the diversification benefit is more marginal. It is rare for the cost size of the equation to win, but for small portfolios, it can make sense to substitute greater U.S. market exposure relative to small cap and end up with a lower cost and still well-diversified portfolio. Of course, as the portfolio grows in assets, the algorithm will add the additional asset class when efficient to do so.

A final example is cash drag. Here, there is once again an optimization to be performed between the implicit cost of holding cash—an asset class that, though stable, typically falls in value due to the presence of inflation—and the costs of trading. For example, investing cash whenever it was present in the account might lead to excessive trading costs. This optimization is performed both for portfolio cash and the cost of dividends.

These are all examples of how digital services can customize portfolios for clients in ways that would be extremely time consuming and likely not economic for humans to do, even though there are gains to be had by doing the work. We can see that this sort of analysis puts powerful analytic capabilities in the hands of investors even with relatively low balances, and results in superior service for them.

At a more abstract level, what is occurring is a large set of cost-benefit equations. Any move in the portfolio is quantified and ultimately presented in dollar terms so that the impact can be assessed.

Every move has both a cost and a benefit to it. Typically, moves in the portfolio can be expected to improve the risk-adjusted return of the portfolio, but these moves will carry some costs due to the frictions of trading. Even superficially free trades that don't carry a commission will be subject to a bid-ask spread and potential tax consequences. Often, the algorithm, which understands all of the costs and benefits of the portfolio, is, in simple terms, "waiting" for a moment when a trade or series of trades can be made that bring multiple benefits to the portfolio at relatively low cost. An example would be a tax loss harvesting trade that can also be used to put dormant cash from a recent string of dividend payments to work and bring a portfolio back to its optimal allocation.

What has been impressive to me over the years the algorithm has been developed is how the sophistication has grown over time in a way that helps customer portfolios. Initially, trades were essentially obvious and easy to follow. Now, the algorithm is able to incorporate so many facets of portfolio construction that a few moves the algorithm makes are no longer obvious at first glance, and you have to actually take a moment, to think through the steps involved. The results are always a better portfolio, but like an Excel sheet dealing with strings of large numbers it's impressive to see the algorithm effortlessly make very powerful decisions, constantly and elegantly bringing portfolios to their optimal state.

KEY TAKEAWAYS

- All portfolios are somewhat unique based on the size of holdings and availability of commission-free funds.
- Dynamic asset selection makes it possible to find the lowest-cost option for a portfolio.
- The key elements of cost for any ETF are the expense ratio, the bid-ask spread, and the trading commission.
- For larger accounts the expense ratio and the bid-ask spreads are the dominant cost, but for smaller accounts the presence of trading commissions can be significant.

Chapter 7

What Software Does Better than People

"In short, software is eating the world."

—Marc Andreessen, Venture Capitalist

S oftware is exceptionally good at some tasks, yet terrible at others. Software is well suited to repeated activities with well-defined principles (fortunately, many areas of financial analysis have these traits). Software doesn't get bored, get sick, or make unintentional mistakes. It doesn't need any vacation days, or leave to work for a competing firm offering more money.

Software and robots generally are playing a growing role in the economy. In areas where precision, number crunching, or strength is needed, computers can do more at lower cost than humans. Computers and robots are playing an increasing role, from self-driving cars to remote oil pipeline inspection.

Of course, as with all prior technology advances, this generates some concerns. The main one is that computers will displace people in the economy. This is known as the "lump of labor" fallacy, because although computers can replace people for certain tasks, people are flexible and can take on new roles. The reason this is true is that computers can reduce the cost of a product or service, just as is occurring with investment management. Fortunately, as basic economics implies, reductions in cost generally see large increases in demand, and with that scale, more supervisory or complementary roles are created. In addition, even in investment management the optimal combination is not complete automation, but a combination of computers and people based on the best skills for the task. For example, as we'll discuss in more detail later in the chapter, computers are well suited to portfolio analysis, but less well suited to client communications, marketing, or new product development. So the growth in computing and robotics may well change the skills that are required for many roles, but it is unlikely to reduce the number of jobs that are needed in the economy.

A good example of how computers can improve productivity comes from agriculture. Previously, farmers would use a consistent approach to a whole field or an entire farm. Now computational analysis based on soil samples and other factors has the potential to provide the right dosage of fertilizer, water, and pesticides to each unique square foot of a farm or even a single plant, based on the accuracy of the global positioning system (GPS). Tractors no longer need a driver, since a tractor managed by computer is able to be more precise in avoiding covering the same area twice or follow precise tracks to protect crops. Now, fertilizer can even be delivered by small multirotor drones.

This new level of insight in agriculture has also shown certain commonly held beliefs to be wrong. For example, it was previously believed that flooding impacted only the area that was immediately flooded; however, detailed computational analysis has shown that a ring of land around flooded areas also sees reduced crop yields. The interaction of detailed inputs and computational analysis is taking farm productivity to new levels.

How Software Helps Investors

There are some analogies to investment management here, whereas before, investment approaches may have been tailored broadly to the individual's wealth and age. Just like bringing a specific approach to a farm or a field, precise portfolio customization down to individual tax lots and other details of individual holdings was a laborious process and simply wasn't done given the high cost relative to the benefit. Software enables individual precision on a vast scale. It is now possible to analyze not just you as an individual, but every position you hold and how to trade those in a way that minimizes cost and maximizes tax efficiency. And that analysis can be performed on an ongoing basis to spot opportunities for benefits such as tax loss harvesting as soon as they emerge.

However, of course, software has no inherent common sense. Every action and rule needs to be completely and comprehensively specified, and all input data needs to be accurate and timely. Fortunately, portfolio construction, customization, and maintenance is a perfect problem for software to address. Optimal portfolio management is both rules based and repetitive. There is such a large a set of rules governing building a well-balanced, low-cost, and tax-smart portfolio that a human may have trouble factoring in everything, and then weighting it appropriately, from wash sale constraints to bid-ask spreads to a customer's unique split between account types, but once correctly configured, software can do it in a heartbeat, and do so every single day the markets are open without failure.

Software also scales well. That means that if something can be done in software once, then doing that same action a million times a day becomes just a matter of processing capacity. This used to be an operational problems with processing capacity. Previously, when businesses had their own physical servers, it was either prohibitively expensive by having a lot of capacity that you wouldn't need most of the time, or risky if demand exceeded server supply for certain hours or days. Fortunately, thanks to cloud based infrastructure, computing can be accessed on demand, just like turning a tap on or off when you need water.

Trading off multiple dimensions of a problem rapidly is something software does well. Conceptually speaking, first you need to assess whether a portfolio has drifted too far from its target allocation across multiple holdings, then you need to assess the tax impacts of trading, then you need to determine if any wash sale constraints are present and whether there is any new cash to incorporate into the portfolio. Then you need to determine the lowest-cost instruments to acquire for the portfolio on a total-cost-of-ownership basis and look for any tax loss harvesting opportunities across holdings. Even this is a relatively simplified view of the portfolio management given the countless edge cases that occur. Performing each of those steps in isolation is reasonably complex, but software can handle all of them in combination instantaneously.

Example: All the Decisions an Algorithm Makes

Consider all of the aspects an advisory algorithm should take into account with a portfolio:

- Basic tests to make sure the data inputs are accurate:
  - Is the deviation from prior inputs within acceptable bounds?
  - Is the incoming data complete?
  - Is there the possibility of duplicate inputs relative to prior inputs?
  - Do secondary sources effectively predict the data? For example, does combining market price changes with yesterday's data provide a similar outcome to today's data set?
- Assessment of opportunity to trade:
  - Is there cash on hand in the account?
  - Is there a need to withdraw client funds?
- How is the portfolio relative to target allocation at the different tiers of the portfolio such as bond-equity split, geographical splits within asset classes, and subasset class levels with different thresholds applied to each?
  - Are there material tax loss harvesting opportunities in any asset classes?
  - Have any positions that were being held until they reached long-term gain status reached long-term capital gains?
- Assessment of optimal trade combination:
  - What are the lowest-cost options among quality funds after taking account of all costs including expense ratios, bid-asks spreads, and commissions?

- Would any proposed trades violate wash sale rules either within the immediate portfolio or across household assets?
- Are all trades material in the context of the portfolio (i.e., avoid moving $10 in the $100,000 portfolio)?
- Does a trade provide a positive portfolio benefit in terms of reduction in fees, greater tax efficiency, or portfolio risk–return improvements after all the costs of trading are reflected?
- Which set of trades best satisfies all of the above constraints from the options available?

Then on top of this individual account process are a large number of system checks to ensure that the right behavior is occurring across the system.

If that sounds complex, bear in mind that the above is a high-level summary of broad rules and that the underlying detail and equations are more sophisticated when expressed mathematically. Nonetheless, the above outlines 14 basic portfolio constraints. Then imagine doing that analysis every day across thousands of portfolios. That's a daunting task for humans, and clearly at that scale some error would likely be introduced if a human were doing it, but that is not an issue for software. More servers can apply the same code repeatedly and achieve the expected results.

Recently, I was discussing with a major asset management firm how they ran their tax loss harvesting operations for clients. This is, broadly, how it was described. It's all hands on deck in December. Our trained financial staff spend weeks during December going through customer accounts and looking for trading opportunities by eye.

This isn't that unusual; in fact, looking for tax loss harvesting opportunities in December is generally the way many still do it. It's better than not doing it all, and a fair amount of the gains from tax loss harvesting can be captured. However, if an opportunity emerges temporarily during the other 11 months of the year, this approach will obviously miss it. That's a sensible trade-off for a human to make, doing tax loss harvesting every month, let alone every day, is enormously time consuming, and though there is a benefit, the time of a financial advisor doing the work would offset the benefit for most individual portfolios.

Compare this annual December human approach to what a computer can do. An effective algorithm can be on the lookout for tax loss harvesting opportunities and anything else that may help improve a portfolio any day the market is open. This occurs without risk of oversight or error.

Of course, algorithmic outputs need to be carefully monitored. Systems of safety lights flag potential issues for human investigation before any trading occurs and the outputs of the algorithm should be compared to what a human would do. It should also be remembered that, unlike humans, computers have no internal notion of ethical behavior, so as computational analysis evolves, computers should also be monitored from that standpoint. As much as decisions produced by an algorithm are very rational, algorithms do ultimately have their own personality, based on how marginal trade-offs are decided and the ultimate weighting of priorities based on forecast time horizons and expected tax consequences.

KEY TAKEAWAYS

- Computers and robots are increasingly being used in many areas of the economy.
- Precision and number crunching at scale are two areas where computers can outperform humans, making them well suited for certain investment management tasks such as portfolio optimization constraints run on a recurring basis.
- Computers can handle multiple investment constraints simultaneously and monitor investment decisions every day the markets are open. This means they are better than humans in some areas of investment portfolio management such as tax loss harvesting.
- The rise of computers in roles such as these likely creates more opportunities for humans in related roles, and ultimately drives down the cost of financial services, increasing demand for them.

Chapter 8

How International Investing Can Smooth Returns

"If you are diversified among different forms of wealth, nations and industries, you'll be safe in the long-run."

—Sir John Templeton

At 85 years old, Jack Bogle is an investing legend. He's the founder and retired CEO of Vanguard. Over the past decades, Vanguard has been pivotal in driving the adoption of low-cost indexing via mutual funds and more recently exchange-traded funds (ETFs).

Indeed, FutureAdvisor uses Vanguard ETFs in constructing portfolios. Vanguard offers low-cost and well-constructed passive investment funds across most key global asset classes.

So it's with concern that I read Bogle's statement on international investing:

The U.S. accounts for about 48 percent (of global market capitalization) and other countries 52 percent. But the top three
markets outside the U.S. are the U.K., Japan and France. What's
the excitement about there? Emerging markets have great
potential, but have fragile sovereigns and fragile institutions.[1]

A historical review shows this logic to be wrong. Imagine it's 1914.
Translating Bogle's logic back a century, you would have argued that
ignoring a little emerging market known as the United States made a lot
of sense. The British empire held sway over about a fifth of the world's
population, and European countries dominated world trade. The United
States appeared "fragile," lacked international influence, maintained a
small army, and ran a distant second to the European economies.

If you chose then to own stocks in the most powerful nation at
the time, Britain, you'd have chosen not to invest in the United States,
missing out on growth of just under 7 percent each year, on average,
after inflation. Investing solely in global powers with strong institutions
ignores the dynamic nature of international development. Recently, the
Chinese economy overtook the United States on a purchasing parity
basis by some measures.

Another important metric looks at how large a stock market is relative to the gross domestic product (GDP) of a country. As of 2015,
broadly speaking, the United States represents half of the global stock
market, but only a quarter of GDP, which suggests the United States
could be expensive and is punching above its weight in stock market
value. This suggests that growth in the United States might be slower
than other nations in the medium term.

Demographics Matter

Another reason to look overseas is demographics. Populations in the
United States and much of the Western world are aging faster than in
emerging markets, and reproducing themselves more slowly, if at all.

The average age in the United States is 37. With a declining birth
rate, the average age is likely to rise over time, leading to a greater
proportion of the population in retirement rather than working.

Conversely, many emerging-market nations have young populations. The average age in Brazil is 30; in India, it's 26. That sets these nations up for reasonable economic growth for the medium term as more of their population will be of working age. Though demographics may seem esoteric, it's actually critical to economic growth, which in turn is critical to stock prices. There are many ways to analyze economic growth, but one relatively simple way is to consider the change in the number of workers and how much each can produce. The change in how much each produces has generally risen by 1.5 percent to 2.5 percent a year, but the number of workers is relatively easy to forecast and can materially increase or decrease this number in a very predictable way. By considering those countries with larger growth of working-age populations, you can have insight into what is likely to drive economic growth and by extension stock market returns over the medium term. Also, I discuss the problem of home bias elsewhere in this book, namely, the issue of investors preferring to invest in their own countries. Assuming that bias remains over time, the growth of incomes in emerging markets, combined with a preference for buying stock in their home country, may offer a further boost to stock markets in emerging markets.

It's important to consider diversification. There are many nations beyond the United States with ample investment opportunities. By holding a broad basket of international stock market exposure, you are more likely to smooth your returns over time rather than pinning your fate to a single economy, however strong it may appear. For example, analysis by academics at the London Business School has shown that even over long periods the fate of different national stock markets can diverge. The best examples of this are China and Russia, which both ceased trading due to nationalization of private assets during the twentieth century, only to return decades later. An internationally diversified portfolio is able to weather these issues. Of course, the United States has been a strong-performing stock market for some time, but it is not certain that this relative advantage will continue indefinitely. Indeed, returns for most national stock markets are relatively similar over the long term, but owning different markets in combination smooths returns.

Diversification Improves Your Industry Mix

Diversification isn't important only on a country level but also on a sector or industry level. As Jose Menchero and Andrei Morozov have shown,[2] sector exposure can be just as important in managing portfolio risk as country exposure at a global level. That is to say, whether you have included, for example, both France and India is just as important to your portfolio as whether you include both mining stocks and technology stocks. Which attribute matters more depends on the region. In emerging markets, countries are more important in driving performance than countries, but in Europe, industry exposure has mattered more for performance than countries. Figure 8.1 shows the extent to which country and industry factors have driven portfolio movements over time, as measured by mean absolute deviation (MAD).

Elroy Dimson and his colleagues at the London Business School have illustrated this clearly looking at FTSE index data. As of 2015,

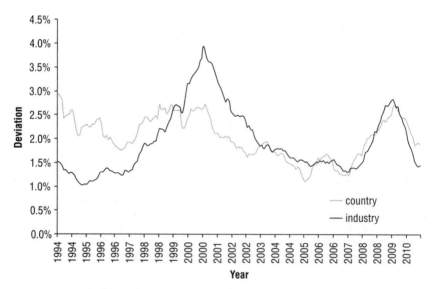

Figure 8.1   Mean Absolute Deviation by Country and Industry

Source: Jose Menchero and Andrei Morozov, "The Relative Strength of Industry and Country Factors in Global Equity Markets." MSCI Research Insight.

if you invested only in the United States, you would be overweight technology and consumer services but underweight telecoms and financials. Some industries are quite specialized to a particular country or region. For example, the majority of alternative energy stocks are in China and Denmark, most mining companies are listed in the United Kingdom and Australia, and the primary producers of leisure goods are in South Korea and Japan. Therefore, country diversification has the potential to smooth returns by exposure to different economic cycles, but also adds more diverse industry exposure than one can obtain by owning a single country in isolation. This is because the major players in most industries are not evenly distributed around the globe and tend to bunch in particular regions or countries. This isn't just a problem for U.S. investors; for example, a U.K.-only investor would have relatively large energy exposure, and a German investor would have large exposure to basic materials companies. If you invest only in a single country, then you are likely be not only taking a bet on a single country that's potentially less efficient than diversifying, but also skewing your sector allocation unnecessarily. Therefore, failing to internationally diversify introduces two risks to your portfolio: (1) you are tied to the macroeconomic cycle of a single country, and (2) you have a selection of industries that omits some of the global economic diversity and overexposes you to certain sectors.

International diversification does introduce potential currency risk. This means that the movement of the U.S. dollar against the currency the stock trades in will impact performance. This impact can be both positive and negative on portfolios and can have a significant annual impact of up to +/− 15 percent on returns of foreign holdings, based on Federal Reserve data. Fortunately, there is a natural hedge to currency movements in the movement of prices of both stocks and bonds. For stocks, if the currency weakens against the dollar, it can promote exports and encourage consumers to spend money domestically. This behavior has the potential to offset stock declines. The reverse is also true: when the U.S. dollar weakens, foreign holdings may do better due to currency movements, but the underlying stocks in those countries may see slower growth due to reduced exports relative to the United States.

KEY TAKEAWAYS

- Historically, the United States has performed relatively well compared to other stock markets, but it is unlikely that this will continue indefinitely.
- International diversification can smooth returns by spreading exposure to business cycles and different sectors of the stock market.
- Adding emerging markets to your portfolio may expose you to favorable demographic trends that may help growth in your portfolio.
- International diversification does add currency risk to a portfolio, though this can be naturally offset over time, by the relative impact on export-led businesses whose fortunes improve when currencies decline.

Notes

1. Jack Bogle, "I Wouldn't Risk Investing Outside the U.S." Bloomberg Business, 2014.
2. Jose Menchero and Andrei Morozov, "The Relative Strength of Industry and Country Factors in Global Equity Markets." MSCI Research Insight.

Chapter 9

The Advantages of Exchange-Traded Funds

"ETFs, in their 25-year history, have become one of the fastest-growing segments of the investment management business."

—Steven Schoenfeld

U p until the 1980s, implementing a low-cost diversified portfolio wasn't easy. Many active funds were trying to beat an index rather than track it, and elsewhere active management, involving trying to pick stocks, seldom delivers repeatable, improved performance. However, the challenge of managing a portfolio yourself, when most benchmarks contain a few hundred to a few thousand instruments was both extremely expensive and extremely time consuming. Investors had two bad options.

The arrival of exchange-traded funds (ETFs) have improved the picture for small investors. They are a cross between stocks and mutual funds, but generally manage to offer the best of both worlds for the long-term investor. Since 1997, the assets devoted to ETFs has doubled roughly every four years, and ETFs now have approximately 10 percent of the assets of mutual funds,[1] which have existed far longer. Actually, the growth in ETFs has coincided with strong growth in mutual fund assets, and the main reduction has been in direct holdings of equities. Essentially, investors are choosing to use funds to gain equity exposure, rather than holding individual company stocks. The growth in ETFs has been rapid in recent years, as Figure 9.1 shows.

The arrival of ETFs has facilitated the creation of digital investment advisors. ETFs have made tax-efficient, low-cost management of portfolios with less than $1 million a reality. Mutual funds with periodic capital gains distributions and complexity in trading relative to stocks are less suited to dynamic portfolio construction than ETFs.

In addition, the bias toward active management across mutual funds creates complexities in constructing complete portfolios because the drift in allocation in mutual funds over time isn't completely transparent. For example, you could own several mutual funds that invest in the U.S. stock market and, in aggregate, because of the independent decisions of

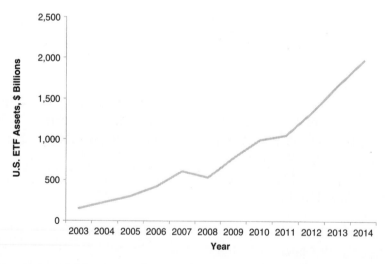

Figure 9.1   ETF Asset Growth

Source: Investment Company Institute

fund managers, have a bias in your portfolio that you weren't aware of that impacts the risk characteristics of the portfolio. For example, if you have a small-, mid-, and large-cap fund and each manager independently bets heavily on tech stocks, your portfolio has a greater tech bias than you might want for portfolio construction purposes and sector diversification, and yet you aren't even aware due to lags in mutual fund reporting. ETFs, however, reporting holdings daily, and many track transparent, predictable benchmarks, so building a portfolio from multiple ETFs doesn't have any hidden potential risks to it.

The Benefits of ETFs

ETFs tend to be cheap to own. Costs are falling all the time, but an ETF can often be 10 times less expensive than an active mutual fund. Since even small costs can add up, that's very helpful to an investor's projected returns. Research has shown that lower-cost investments generally outperform high-cost ones, simply because outperforming the markets is so hard to do, so with an active fund, you are left with average performance less fees. Given that we can predict fees in advance, they tend to be the best predictor of performance. Declining fees therefore lead to better prospective returns for investors. Since ETFs tend to be low fee, they tend to have higher performance as a result.

ETFs are also extremely liquid. They trade on exchanges just like stocks, and since they typically contain many individual instruments in fixed ratios, more can be created as needed if volume doesn't meet demand, and vice versa if demand for the ETF falls. The underlying value of the ETF is typically calculated every 15 seconds so that any premium or discount to its underlying assets can be assessed. Rather than fire sale pricing, the ETFs can simply be converted back into the underlying stocks at scale. Essentially, ETFs are free to tap into the liquidity of the markets they track. This means that even if an ETF is relatively small, if it tracks a large market, then it can be quite liquid. Generally, an ETF can be created by an authorized participant assembling "creation units" from the constituent assets behind the ETF, which typically create a number of shares in the tens or hundreds of thousands. These shares can then either be held by the authorized participant or sold to clients typically through an exchange, though a direct transition is with a larger client is also possible.

In-Kind Transfers

This process of creating ETFs by purchasing the underlying shares in the appropriate mix also indirectly leads to tax efficiency for ETFs through a process called *in-kind transfers.*

In-kind transfers help ETFs avoid passing taxes onto investors in most cases. ETFs are able to do this because large institutions create shares in ETFs by purchasing a basket of underlying securities. For example, for each Standard & Poor's (S&P) 500 ETF, a financial institution purchases the 500 shares in the S&P 500 and passes on shares in the ETF that can be sold. When shares are sold, the reverse happens. Now, the shares that are chosen to be transferred can be selected based on their tax lots. Shares with large capital gains can be transferred out using this process and exchanged for ETF shares rather than sold. This in-kind transfer is exactly that—a transfer—and doesn't involve any selling of the underlying shares and can be used to remove holdings that would otherwise be significantly taxed if they were sold. Figure 9.2 shows how this process operates.

Conversely, mutual funds can often result in the passing on of taxable gains that are messy for the investor. First, taxable gains are undesirable in the first place. But second and more importantly, the distribution of gains may not match the holding period of the mutual fund. This could

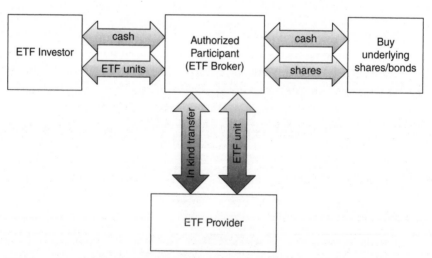

Figure 9.2   ETF Creation and Redemption Process

mean that if you hold a mutual fund for only a relatively short period, you may get lucky and not receive any capital gains, but if you're unlucky, you may receive one despite only holding the fund temporarily. Of course, for any longer-term investor holding for several years it's likely that the holding period and the capital gain will correspond, but regardless, a mutual fund is still likely to be a less tax-efficient structure than an ETF.

This means that, according to Investment Company Institute data, in 2013 about half of mutual funds passed on capital gains to investors, but around 1 ETF in 25 did. Furthermore, those ETFs that paid out capital gains tend to follow leveraged strategies or hold bonds or commodities; for an ETF focused on conventional equities to have a capital gain was rare.

The generally superior tax efficiency of ETFs has been quantified at 0.35 percent of a post-tax performance gain a year, on average, and that's even before the fact that mutual funds are more expensive and more problematic instruments to use as building blocks of larger, aggregate portfolios.

Mutual funds can also have additional fees, such as load fees when you buy or when you sell. These fees are pretty outrageous, since it's not as if buying or selling the mutual fund entails any more real work for anyone, and like all fees in finance, they are generally declining; nonetheless, with ETFs you typically pay only an expense ratio for holding the fund. An expense ratio is expressed as a percentage of the value of the fund over a year, so for a fund with an expense ratio of 0.20 percent, if you invested $10,000 for a year, you'd pay $20 in expense. If you held it for six months, the cost would be $10.

The Risks of ETFs

Of course, ETFs are not all plain sailing. The market for ETFs is innovating all the time, and like all innovation, there are good and bad results. Some ETFs can be very small, with limited track records, relatively poor liquidity, and high trading costs.

There is also a fundamental risk with certain ETFs that the U.S. Treasury has identified in that ETFs are extremely transparent and liquid instruments, but if they are constructed from instruments that do not trade so frequently, such as less liquid debt instruments, risks may emerge. An ETF is expected to offer constant liquidity, but if markets for an underlying instrument dry up, then an ETF may behave in unexpected ways, not matching the performance of the underlying basket of investments because the ETFs has to offer liquidity.

This is unlikely to be a broad issue for ETFs based on broad sets of stocks and bonds such as the ones we select at FutureAdvisor, but as ETFs become more exotic and include instruments that do not trade daily and do not have deep, liquid markets, then their possible risks will emerge at times of market stress or unexpected events. There are two historical examples that show the potential for this, though both are relatively limited in scope for longer-term investors.

During the Arab Spring uprising of 2011 in Egypt, the Egyptian stock market closed, yet an Egyptian ETF on the U.S. market continued to trade. It rose over 3 percent above its previous net asset value and became the proxy for the Egyptian market while the Egyptian market itself was closed. A similar process occurred during summer 2015 when the Greek stock market was closed, along with Greek banks, while bailout negotiations were conducted. Greek ETFs continued to trade during this period.

Separately, during the 2010 Flash Crash, when markets fell temporarily and rapidly, many ETFs were caught up in the frenzy, with some falling more than the stocks they represented. This is the cost of liquidity. ETFs are trading when the markets are open and hence can experience volatility. Generally, deviations from net asset value are limited for ETFs and are unlikely to be a concern for long-term investors, but for short-term traders these occasional events are noteworthy.

It should be noted that mutual funds themselves can face similar risks. For example, with the collapse of Lehman Brothers in 2008, money market funds, which were previously considered an extremely low-risk investment, traded below par due to market events—an outcome few would have expected.

Also, not all ETFs meet the needs of a long-term investor, some leveraged ETFs are constructed to provide triple the return of the S&P 500 on a daily basis. This can be done over the course of a single trading day, but the probable fall in value between days means that even if the markets are going up, any investor for the longer term in these instruments is likely to lose money. This isn't to say that these instruments are unsustainable, just that they are trading instruments and unsuitable for longer-term investor. There is also some risk that an investor doesn't understand what they are buying, one might expect a 2× leverage fund to yield double the return of the S&P 500 (for example), but that's not what happens over the longer term.

Securities Lending Policies

When you consider an ETF, it's important to take account of securities lending policies. ETFs that engage in prudent securities lending can reduce the burden of investment management fees and enhance your returns. Remarkably, some low-fee ETFs can actually beat their benchmarks because of securities lending policies. This essentially makes them free to own. Of course, this isn't true for all ETFs, but some that hold stocks that are hard to borrow and hence attract higher lending fees can do well. In fact, some ETFs such as the Vanguard Small Cap ETF (VB) have done so over a period of many years.

It's important to understand how ETFs and securities lending work. An ETF is, in essence, a stock that encompasses a group of assets. An ETF can include a group of bonds or stocks designed to meet an investment objective or track an index. Although an ETF encompasses a group of assets, it acts like a single stock and is bought, sold, and traded on the stock market. This means that its total value fluctuates daily on an exchange.

Securities lending for an ETF works in the following way. Your ETF agrees to lend a specific stock to a third party in exchange for collateral. The ETF provider receives a fee in return for lending the stock and can also earn a return on the collateral it holds while the stock is lent. There are two main risks involved: (1) that the third party fails to return the stock, and (2) that the collateral against the loan falls in value. Both risks can be managed by an effective trading desk. And if you're wondering about the motivation of the third party in the transaction, they are likely a short seller, hoping the stock will fall in value, so that the stock they return to close out the transaction is worth less than at the time they borrowed it.

The amount of securities lending profits that ETF sponsors pass onto ETF investors varies, but appears to be increasing. As of the start of 2014, some ETF products returned 70 percent to 75 percent of securities lending revenue to investors. Others return 100 percent of securities lending proceeds to investors after their costs. As Dave Nadig of ETF .com argues, the difference isn't just in the revenue/profit split, which is calculated in a slightly different way by the different firms; it's also in the policies for lending. Some firms appear to lend more broadly, hence increasing potential lending returns, but also raising the risk level slightly, whereas others may be more selective in identifying lending opportunities with greater profitability.

So what are some of the funds that benefit most from securities lending? As I mentioned previously, the Vanguard Small Cap ETF (VB) has historically eliminated its costs with securities lending and is a constituent of many FutureAdvisor customer portfolios. The Vanguard Small Cap Growth ETF (VBK) has outperformed its benchmark on a 10-year view but not over the past year. iShares Russell 2000 ETF (IWM), along with the growth-tilted variant (IWO), has beaten its benchmark for the past three calendar years, though interestingly the value-tilted sibling (IWN) has not. Turning to State Street, the SPDR S&P 600 Small Cap ETF (SLY) has seen benchmark outperformance since inception, but this outperformance appears less consistent year to year.

Generally, it appears that the small-cap and growth-oriented funds benefit from securities lending due to higher lending fees for the stocks that they hold. It is important to note that the benefit of securities lending does not appear to carry over to active mutual funds, though a majority do engage in the practice. A working paper by Evans, Ferreira, and Prado concludes that active funds that engage in securities lending tend to underperform similar funds by a significant amount.[2] This may be due to selection effects, since the securities which attract significant lending fees are more likely to fall in price. The authors imply that these stocks should be sold rather than lent. However, this is not an issue for index funds that are tracking a defined benchmark and hence have no stock selection decisions to make.

As with everything in life, the fact that something is free doesn't necessarily mean you need to have it. There is some minor risk involved in lending activities. In the future, changes in the fees for securities lending or many other factors could impact these ETFs. Nonetheless, if you are looking at gaining small-capitalization exposure in your portfolio, consider an ETF that is both low cost and engages in securities lending as a potential way to enhance your returns.

In addition, ETFs can implement any strategy, but obviously, all strategies make sense after costs. ETFs are a way to build a portfolio, but using ETFs doesn't guarantee a robust portfolio—just one that may be cheaper and more diversified than alternatives. Just like building a house from brick is a good idea, but using brick doesn't mean that your house won't be ugly.

KEY TAKEAWAYS

- ETFs are a fast-growing, low-cost, transparent, and liquid asset class.
- Because of their liquidity, they can trade when the underlying instruments do not, which can create both opportunity and risk.
- ETFs offer an appropriate and tax-efficient vehicle for digital advisors to build client portfolios.

Notes

1. Investment Company Institute, "Investment Company Factbook," 2015; Joanne M. Hill, Dave Nadig, and Matt Hougan, "A Comprehensive Guide to ETFs," CFA Institute Research Foundation, 2015.
2. Richard B. Evans, Miguel A. Ferreira, and Melissa Porras Prado, "Fund Performance and Equity Lending: Why Lend What You Can Sell?" 2014.

Chapter 10

The Triumph of Low-Cost Investing

How Paying Less Gets You More

"It is remarkable how much long-term advantage people like us have gotten by trying to be consistently not stupid, instead of trying to be very intelligent."

—Charlie Munger

I n 2015, Europe's largest daily newspaper, *Bild of Germany*, ran a front-page story with the headline "Slim by chocolate!" that suggested the latest new diet fad. The story was then picked up by media outlets across the world from the *Times of India* to an Australian morning talk show. A team of German researchers at the Institute of Diet and Health had come up with a weight-loss formula that was both

easy to implement and effective. Chocolate was the weight-loss accel-
erator that the world had been looking for.

The problem was that the research wasn't robust. Journalist John
Bohannon was proving a point—pretty successfully, it turned out. He
was proving that there are a lot of bad data, and people (and indeed
journalists) don't often separate the wheat from the chaff. John and his
team recruited 15 people and measured 18 different variables (weight,
cholesterol, sodium, blood protein levels, sleep quality, well-being, etc.)
over three weeks. This gave them a slightly better than 60 percent chance
of finding a significant data point, even if the data were random, and in
fact they found two to help prove their point.

Fooled by Randomness

The research was done to show that findings that look robust can carry
limited actual meaning. The same is true of mutual funds. The Investment Company Institute (ICI) Factbook catalogued over 7,000 mutual
funds in the United States as of 2013. By pure statistics, around half of
those should do better than average, some much better. Equally, some
should do worse than average, and some much worse.

However, these outcomes will be relatively random, it doesn't mean
that the good performers are entitled to command high fees. Mutual
fund performance has attracted a lot of attention from academics in
studies of different funds over different time periods.

In fact, rather alarmingly, the average mutual fund generally under-
performs its benchmark by 0.89 percent[1] a year, based on an examination of 636 mutual funds between 1985 and 1989. A similar study of
large pension plans between 1974 and 1983 founds that active managers
underperformed passive ones by 1.10 percent a year, due mainly to poor
market timing and, to a lesser extent, poor security selection.[2] Another
study[3] looks at mutual funds from 1974 to 1995 and finds underperformance of passive funds of 1 percent per year. However, this return is de-
composed to find that stock picking is, in isolation, positive, but dragged
down by fees and transaction costs. The author then argues that stock
picking is a positive activity. This is certainly at the more optimistic end
of interpretations because these funds are still losing money for investors,
but certainly if mutual funds became free and trading costs were zero,

the value of active management may be worth reconsidering in some cases. This is a similar outcome to one of the first analyses done on this topic in 1996,[4] finding that mutual funds underperform by 0.65 percent a year on average, again with any stock-picking advantage more than offset by high fees. Reinforcing this result, another study looked at the performance of mutual fund's holdings relative to the performance of the fund, and one of the key findings was that transaction costs reduced performance by 2.5 percent a year.[5]

In looking at different active funds over different time periods, it appears that you can lose 0.6 percent to 1.1 percent of your money each year by picking an active fund relative to the market. In 2014, active mutual funds charged on average 0.75 percent more a year than an equivalent passive fund.[6] We also should be a little cautious about the studies that find a benefit to active fund's stock picking, even before fees. The reason is based in statistics. On average, your return to stock picking should be around zero, so if in the four studies we've looked at we find two showing a slight benefit to stock picking and two showing a slight cost, then that's what you may expect. The market is fairly efficient, so finding stocks that will outperform is just as hard as finding stocks that will underperform. For example, if you were a consistently bad stock picker, someone could just buy all the stocks you don't own and beat the market. These studies show that stock picking just introduces random variation into your portfolio. With stocking picking you may, randomly, come out slightly ahead; you may, again randomly, come out slightly behind, but the fees and costs will certainly drag down your performance, as all four of the studies show.

We did our own analysis at FutureAdvisor of Standard & Poor's (S&P) 500 benchmarked funds over the 2013–2014 period, and though the market was up strongly, the impact of fees was as clear as the majority of studies have shown (see Figure 10.1).

In fact, just as in the chocolate example, Kothari and Werner[7] find that in creating random samples of 50 stocks to mimic mutual funds they are able to find some significantly outperforming benchmarks, even though the portfolios are entirely random and devoid of any skill. This suggests that the tests used to assess mutual fund performance might be easier than they are intended to be and the bar is lower than it should be, even though most mutual funds fail to clear it.

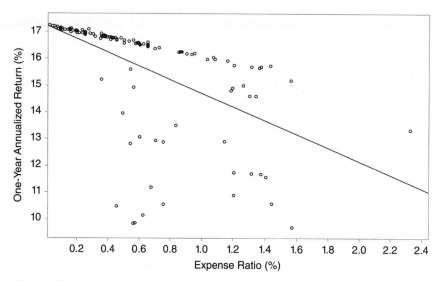

Figure 10.1   Fees vs. Performance for S&P 500 Benchmarked Funds, 2-13-2014
Source: FutureAdvisor

There are so many funds out there that there will always be firms with what appears to be a strong track record that garner attention, and just as it's tempting to believe that a tempting diet fad may help you lose weight, maybe a talented fund manager can help you beat the market. Unfortunately, in both cases you may be misled, and neither your wallet not your waistline is likely to move in the direction you hope.

Still, aside from the cold, hard facts, it remains a tempting message: get more, pay less. This promise has people jumping in most areas of life—a bottle of Domaine Leroy Musigny Grand Cru for the price of Two-Buck Chuck, a penthouse suite instead of a motel room, a free flight upgrade to first class. All of these decisions are no-brainers.

A Triumph of Marketing over Results

It appears to be in part due to the triumph of marketing over results in finance. There is a general expectation that smart people in suits will do a great job managing investments. However, the sad truth is that numerous studies have shown investment results to be poor. As we've just seen, study after study has shown that paying more gets you less in investing.

The intuition behind this is that in investing what you pay is directly at odds with what you are looking to buy. Investing is generally about making more money, but the more you pay, the less money you have. This central truth has been echoed in research papers from leading academics at the most prestigious institutions.

The average mutual fund charges 1.3 percent in fees. This cost goes toward paying the salaries of fund managers, administrative expenses, brokerage commissions, and even advertising. Theoretically, one might think active management leads to higher returns. That is not the case.

A growing body of evidence shows that higher expense funds do not, on average, perform better than lower expense funds. In fact, the average actively managed fund loses to a low-cost index fund, free of all fees and expenses. The groundbreaking study on this topic came from Michael Jensen at Harvard, who looked at the performance of 115 mutual funds and found that none did better than he would have expected by random chance.[8] He did find that mutual funds were helpful in diversifying investors' stock exposure but that their ability to beat the market, even before the fees charged to clients were taken into account, was weak. "Thus on average the funds apparently were not quite successful enough in their trading activities to recoup even their brokerage expenses."

Mark Carhart, in *The Journal of Finance* in 1997,[9] reached a similar conclusion, finding that expenses have a significant impact on mutual fund performance. A 1 percent increase in expense ratio reduces fund performance by 1.54 percent. However, for certain kinds of fees, it's even worse. Load fees can reduce fund performance by 0.80 percent even before the impact of the load fees themselves are taken into account. His research also found that the degree of trading can also drive down returns to investors, with every 1 percent increase in turnover driving down returns. Basically, the broad mutual fund database and subsequent analysis that Carhart performs suggests that cheaper mutual funds, with less turnover and no load fees, perform better for investors, on average. Fortunately, load fees are declining in significance in the industry over time, and though mutual funds with additional sales fees or load fees still do exist, as of 2014, 64 percent of new money is going into funds that have no sales fees, up from 50 percent in 2005.[10]

Fund fees and performance are inversely, and clearly, linked. When Morningstar tested the ability of expense ratios and its star rating system to predict fund performance, it found that low fees are actually a superior indicator of performance. "In every single time period and data point tested, low-cost funds beat high-cost funds," the report said. "Expense ratios are strong predictors of performance. In every asset class over every time period, the cheapest quintile produced higher total returns than the most expensive quintile."

Investors in a low-fee fund not only earn higher returns but also save more money. The lower your costs, the greater your share of an invest-ment's return. Vanguard looked at the impact of expenses of a portfolio with a starting value of $100,000 over the course of 30 years, which grows an average of 6 percent annually. "In the low-cost scenario, the investor pays 0.25 percent of assets every year, whereas in the high-cost scenario, the investor pays 0.90 percent," the research said. "The potential impact on the portfolio balances over three decades is striking—a differ-ence of almost $100,000 between the low-cost and high-cost scenarios."

In an article titled "The Arithmetic of Investment Expenses,"[11] Nobel Prize winning Stanford Professor William F. Sharpe estimated that a per-son saving for retirement who chooses low-cost investments could save 30 percent more money, and have a standard of living throughout retire-ment more than 20 percent higher, than that of a comparable investor in high-cost investments. Sharpe argues that the apparently low expense ratios understate the true cost of fees to investors, and the terminal wealth ratio (TWR) is a superior system for considering the impact of fees on investors. High-fee funds mean you are paying more to get less in return. This, as any rational consumer or investor can tell you, makes no sense.

Even Warren Buffett, the most famous investor in the world, advocates investing in low-cost S&P funds when he details how his family should manage their inheritance. As he wrote in his 2014 letter to shareholders:[12]

> Huge institutional investors, viewed as a group, have long under-
> performed the unsophisticated index-fund investor who simply
> sits tight for decades. A major reason has been fees.

Though the bulk of research has shown that lower-cost and pas-sive funds do better on average, some critics have argued it is unfair to combine low cost and passive as one. For example, Dylan Minor has shown that for certain time periods active management can perform well.[13] However, this is true only when it is low cost, and generally active management is a high-cost activity. If in the future active managers offer low-cost services, they may be able to outperform passive indexes.

However, at the moment, finding an active manager able to offer services on a similar cost basis to a low-cost mutual fund is unlikely. There are also some implementation issues in that exchange-traded funds (ETFs) have some inherent tax efficiency to them due to in-kind transfers. However, the transparency and liquidity that ETFs offer may not be conducive to active management.

The second argument is that if the world of investing shifts to being fundamentally passive, then active investing will become easier. That is to say, it's a lot easier to find $10 lying in the street if no one else is looking for it. That may be true logically, but we are far from that today. Currently, only 30 percent of funds are passive versus 70 percent active in the United States, and in Europe the split is 10 percent passive to 90 percent active. If passive continues to grow so that it is a majority of the market, then maybe active management will become more compelling, but, as studies have shown, only if it is done at much lower cost than today. Basically, though, active versus passive is an interesting debate. Data suggest that low cost versus high cost is the real driver of performance, and for the time being most active funds are firmly in the high-cost camp.

There may also be one final nail of the coffin in the active management industry. If portfolio tilts to value and small cap, for example, do outperform the market, as research suggests they have historically, then the broader adoption of these techniques may make active management even harder, even if active management costs do fall. In a recent book,[14] Larry Swedroe and Andrew Berkin argue that many active managers used factor exposure to achieve their investment results, either directly or inadvertently, for example, a bias toward the value factor in constructing portfolios. This means that active managers, as much as they were picking stocks, were really just investing more in cheaper companies (the value factor), among other factors. Now, as we have seen, those results weren't terribly impressive in the first place.

So, now the factors that active managers have used historically, and may have been a good source of their returns, are captured by low-cost ETFs, which potentially makes it even harder for active managers to beat the markets, since lower-cost ETFs may have captured the part of their strategies that offered the greatest value to clients.

Quality and cost may be linked when it comes to wine or hotels; however, when it comes to choosing an investment fund, you don't get more for paying more. In this case, the less you pay, the more you save. Those thousands upon thousands of dollars will serve you far better working for you in a retirement account than frittered away on fees.

KEY TAKEAWAYS

- Numerous studies have shown that mutual funds tend to underperform the stock market.
- This is not necessarily because they tend to pick stocks poorly. If anything, stock picking is random and sometimes helps performance and sometimes hurts it. This is what you would logically expect with a large number of funds competing in a reasonably efficient market.
- However, the fees charged by mutual funds and transactions do significantly reduce returns and even during periods where mutual funds happen to do well on stock picking, fees and transaction costs more than offset the benefit, on average.

Notes

1. William F. Sharpe, "Asset Allocation: Management Style and Performance Measurement." *Journal of Portfolio Management* 18(2) (1992): 7–19.
2. Gary P. Brinson, L. Randolph Hood, and Gilbert L. Beebower, "Determinants of Portfolio Performance," *Financial Analysts Journal* (January–February 1995): 133–138.
3. Russ Wermers, "Mutual Fund Performance: An Empirical Decomposition into Stock-Picking Talent, Style, Transactions Costs, and Expenses." *The Journal of Finance* 55(4) (2000): 1655–1703.
4. Martin J. Gruber, "Another Puzzle: The Growth in Actively Managed Mutual Funds." *The Journal of Finance* 51(3) (July 1996): 783–810.

5. Mark Grinblatt and Sheridan Titman, "Mutual Fund Performance: An Analysis of Quarterly Portfolio Holdings." *Journal of Business* 62(3) (1989): 393–416.
6. Investment Company Institute, "Investment Company Factbook," 2014.
7. S. P. Kothari and Jerold B. Warner, "Measuring Long-Horizon Security Price Performance." *Journal of Financial Economics* 43 (1997): 301–339.
8. Michael C. Jensen, "The Performance of Mutual Funds in the Period 1945–1964." *The Journal of Finance* 23(2) (May 1968): 389–416.
9. Mark Carhart, M., "On Persistence in Mutual Fund Performance." *The Journal of Finance* 52(1) (March 1997): 57–82.
10. Investment Company Institute, "Investment Company Factbook," 2014.
11. William F. Sharpe, "The Arithmetic of Investment Expenses." *Financial Analysts' Journal* 69 (2) (2013): 34–41.
12. Warren Buffett, Letter to shareholders of Berkshire Hathaway, 2014.
13. Dylan B. Minor, "Beware of Index Fund Fundamentalists." *The Journal of Portfolio Management* 27(4) (2001): 45–50.
14. Larry Swedroe and Andrew Berkin, *The Incredible Shrinking Alpha*. BAM ALLIANCE Press, 2015.

Chapter 11

Learning from Nobel Prize Winners

"If I have seen further it is by standing on the shoulders of giants."

—Isaac Newton

I n investing there is no shortage of freely available good ideas. Unfortunately, there are many publicly available bad ideas as well. For example, the news media is more interested in creating an attention-grabbing story than a truly robust analysis. The good news is that there are some tests we can use to keep us on the right track by separating the signal from the noise.

One of the best checks for quality of academic thinking is peer-reviewed academic research. Any academic paper in a journal is reviewed by others before publication and then cited in subsequent papers according to its usefulness. Not all journals are peer reviewed, but most of the leading ones are. Citations can also be a useful metric for quality of academic thinking—thinking that is cited by other academics is often high quality. Of course, these papers are often less fun to read than the latest news stories, but they contain ideas and concepts with rigorous academic thinking and are more likely to be useful to an investor as a result.

The very best thinking ultimately receives the Nobel Prize, often after the research has had a chance to be tested after a decade or two. That doesn't mean Nobel Prize–winning thinking is bulletproof. It still may be disproved or modified at some time in the future, but you stand a pretty good chance of having a robust portfolio if you're building it on Nobel Prize–winning concepts. Ideas that have won the Nobel Prize have cleared a much higher hurdle than the typical investment fad.

Here's a look back at some of the Nobel Prize winners in economics and how you can put their insights to use in your portfolio. Of course, this is a selective list. Many economists who haven't won the Nobel Prize contributed important ideas to investment thinking that aren't on the list below. In addition, the Nobel Prize winner is typically awarded for a broad body of work, and here we just examine the thinking that's relevant to financial markets and investment, often disregarding some critical economic thought in the process, albeit thought that doesn't directly accrue to investment success.

Milton Friedman, 1976

Milton Friedman was a prominent economist across many fields of research, and his views on markets weren't the central part of his work, given that he produced important insight across many areas. Nonetheless, he had a very logical view on market efficiency, which highlights a central paradox. As he said in one quote when interviewed by Justin Fox, "Warren Buffett proves that there's not an efficient market, and yet Warren Buffett makes the market efficient." This is a very rational way to approach market efficiency. The markets are not absolutely perfect and, at the margin, people can earn a profit improving them. However, the very fact that people like Warren Buffett are out there looking for mispriced securities makes it then harder for others to find mispriced securities.

Friedman's thinking opens the door to the idea that the markets are hard to beat but are not completely perfect; hence, there is the potential opportunity for asset allocation decisions to help returns relative to risk.

James Tobin, 1981

James Tobin developed a powerful insight for market valuation. He looked at the value of the stock market relative to its book value. Book value is an accounting measure of the total assets of a business after liabilities are deducted. This is an accounting measure of what a company's stock might be worth based on its balance sheet. He identified that if a stock were trading for more than the value of its net assets, then it would be rational to buy a similar set of assets rather than buy the stock. So, for example, if a company that owns a factory making toys is trading significantly more than its book value, then an investor might be better served by constructing a similar toy factory directly rather than buying the stock, because building the toy factory would be a cheaper way to get to the same result. Equally, if a stock traded for less than its net assets, then buying the stock was the rational course. Both of these actions would serve to bring a stock or a stock market back into line with its book value, and hence book value provided a reasonable metric of valuation.

Of course, there are also some accounting considerations with this approach, since accounting book value may not always equal true replacement cost due to depreciation and inflation, but the insight is a powerful one in offering a clear logical principle to determine fair value for stocks. One can look at the value of a company or an entire market and gain insights into its long-term valuation. If the ratio of stock value to book value exceeds 1, then the stock might be overvalued; if the book value is adjusted to capture the true replacement value of all assets, then the company is overvalued according to the same argument.

Building on Friedman's insight, Tobin offers a way to determine when markets might be particularly attractive or expensive.

Harry Markowitz, 1990

Harry Markowitz won the Nobel Prize in 1990 for something called Modern Portfolio Theory. The basic idea is that a portfolio can be more, or less, than the sum of its parts. Optimizing a portfolio is likely to result in better performance for investors. For example, stocks and bonds are both risky in their own way, but holding them together can cancel out some of the risk of both. Hence, you should think about assets in a portfolio in combination, and doing so may lead to better investment performance.

Markowitz's insights led to the creation of broadly inclusive portfolios, rather than just betting on a handful of assets or markets, because each asset class has some unique aspects to it. For example, internationally diversified portfolios combining different countries have the potential to offer smoother returns because the highs and lows of individual country returns are essentially averaged out and the returns to different global equity markets over the long term are similar.

Markowitz's insight leads to the view that strong portfolios incorporate a broad range of assets to improve risk and return. Of course, behind the scenes individual components of the asset class may be moving up or down quite dramatically, but at the portfolio level, because all investments have some unique characteristics to them, returns will be smoother. One way to think about this is that rather than owning your own home, which is exposed to a number of specific risks such as earthquakes, fire, flooding, or other disasters, you instead own a very small share of every home in America. Of course, each year bad things will happen to a relatively small number of homes, but overall your returns will be much smoother by owning a large number of houses.

Of course, Markowitz's work is deeply mathematical, which is both a strength and a weakness. It requires returns and risk for each asset class to be specified as well as the relationship between them. In practice, though long-term returns over decades might be forecast with some reasonable predictive power (though even here there is a lot of noise that isn't forecastable), measuring risk and the relationships between assets is a harder challenge. Over time, the risk characteristics of an investment and its relationship to others can change materially. This means that Markowitz's work is theoretically valid, but detailed implementation creates a number of challenges.

William Sharpe, 1990

Bill Sharpe provided many contributions to financial theory, but one especially relevant one was how it is mathematically impossible for an average active investor to outperform. This is because the performance of investors must equal the performance of the market. This is nothing more than saying that, in total, everyone in the market must earn the average market return. Another way to think about this is that every time you buy or sell a stock, there is someone on the other side of that trade who is selling for your purchase to occur or buying so that you can sell. This means that in aggregate, investors must receive the market's rate of return and it cannot be beaten.

However, active investors also charge fees, which reduce return. So an average investor will earn the market's return, but if a 2 percent fee is charged, then they'll earn the market's return less 2 percent. As a result, a typical investor would be expected to match the market's return before fees and lose money after fees. That's not to say that active managers cannot outperform, but for any outperformance of the market, there must also be corresponding underperformance of the market, and the average investor will ultimately trail the market.

Daniel Kahnemann, 2002

Daniel Kahnemann was instrumental in showing, through a series of experiments, that people were not as logical or as rational as economic theory suggested. This was important research in reconciling the idea that markets sometimes drifted from rational valuations and showed, using empirical models of human behavior, why such inefficiency may occur. Kahnemann's contribution helped offer a more complete view of how markets operate.

Eugene Fama and Robert Shiller, 2013

Eugene Fama developed the factor-based model of the markets. This showed that if you invest in certain factors such as value or small cap, then over time you have the potential to earn an excess return in a portfolio. Interestingly, having previously been a defender of market efficiency, Fama's research showed that the markets were not as efficient as many had previously imagined. Robert Shiller is famous for demonstrating that the markets were overvalued in 2000 and also suggesting that the housing market was overheated in 2007–2008. Both of these assessments proved to be correct, and Shiller provided robust metrics to assess longer-term market value, loosely following the approach of James

Tobin. In the Shiller 10-year PE, the market value is assessed relative to a decade of earnings history to avoid excessive focus on a good or bad short-term environment.

KEY TAKEAWAYS

- Peer-reviewed and Nobel Prize–winning research can form a robust basis for managing an investment portfolio.
- Markowitz demonstrated how combining different assets can improve the risk and return aspects of a portfolio, even if some of the individual assets might appear unattractive.
- The concept of completely efficient markets can be challenged from multiple angles, including behavioral finance and tilts to value and small cap.
- Despite these criticisms, the markets appear to remain largely efficient.

Chapter 12

The Costs of Being Active

Once in the dear dead days beyond recall, an out-of-town visitor was being shown the wonders of the New York financial district. When the party arrived at the Battery, one of his guides indicated some handsome ships riding at anchor. He said, "Look, those are the bankers' and brokers' yachts."
"Where are the customers' yachts?" Asked the naïve visitor.
> —Fred Schwed, *Where Are The Customers' Yachts?*, 1940

As we discussed in Chapter 10, returns to mutual funds are generally weaker than the markets they benchmark against, mainly because costs of tractions and expense ratios drag down costs. However, there is now a further issue with mutual funds, according to the recent research of Antti Petajisto, formerly of Yale University and now at Blackrock.[1]

The problem is this: The point of owning a mutual fund is paying a team of analysts to pick stocks on your behalf, but according to this research, a significant group of mutual funds are no more than "closet indexers,"[2] closer to following the market than trying to beat it. This matters because not only are you paying a high fee, but you aren't getting what you might expect. It's a little like paying up for Gucci loafers and then discovering that the shoes you received are remarkably similar to a pair from Target.

The average mutual fund in the study had a fee of 1.29 percent a year, whereas a passive exchange-traded fund (ETF) that tracks U.S. stock can currently be held for as little as 0.05 percent a year. So the average active fund costs 25 times more than a passive ETF. Though costs for both active and passive funds have fallen in a few cases since the study and continue to be on broad decline, 25 times is a pretty steep price premium. To put that in perspective bear in mind that a Porsche 911 is "only" 5 times the cost of a Toyota Camry, or flying first class is normally 3 to 6 times the cost of an economy seat. Or a very expensive hotel room can run to 6 times the cost of a cheap motel. So 25 times is a substantial premium to pay for just about anything that you purchase.

However, the kicker here is that this and other data suggest that performance of passive ETFs is superior, precisely because of their lower fees. To be clear, the product that costs 25 times as much does worse. It's like a Porsche that's slower than a Camry, a middle seat with limited legroom in first class, or a top hotel room with stains on the carpet. Active funds cost you money but generally don't deliver.

Unlike with cars, flights, or shoes, in finance the fees you pay matter a great deal since they eat into your savings. If you find that result surprising, remember that even Morningstar has come to the same conclusion, finding low fees to be a superior indicator of performance than their very own star rating system. Basically, even before this issue, active funds tend to underperform the index by −0.41 percent a year on average after costs, so you tend to end up behind with active funds based on the data, even before dealing with the potential risk and excessive fees of owning a closet tracker.

The Cost of Closet Indexing

The active fund issue is this. For the 180 funds that are identified as closet indexers, which is about 16 percent of all U.S. equity funds studied, the active share is 59 percent and the average fee is 1.04 percent.

To dive into math for a moment, this means that you are actually paying 1.76 percent for the proportion of the portfolio that is actively managed. This is because the remaining 41 percent of the fund is almost certainly no better than a tracker, and you could own that tracker part of the portfolio for 0.05 percent. In essence, many active funds aren't picking enough stocks in large enough proportions to deviate from their benchmark in a meaningful way. That's not surprising, even the best stock pickers are very selective in what they hit. One of Warren Buffett's tenets as an investor is that he doesn't have to swing at every pitch, by taking a view on every investment that comes across his desk; if he did, his performance would, presumably, be a lot worse. As a result, their performance is very likely to resemble that of the index, which is not the point of owning an active fund. However, the challenge of being a stock picker is that you will have a strong view on only a subset of stocks.

So we now have two problems. Active funds underperform the index, but several of them appear to be expensive index trackers. The Growth Fund of America (AGTHX) is one example, according the research. It is an extremely large fund with over $140 billion in assets per recent reports. However, its active share was relatively low, at under 60 percent as of 2009, and hence the fees charged are relatively high given how much of the fund tracks the index based on Petajisto's research. This is perhaps not surprising, as the fund with $140 billion in assets has such significant market impact that it is extremely challenging to be sufficiently agile to move into and out of stocks without adversely impacting their price. Nonetheless, it appears that you save money and obtain a similar result with a passive ETF, or if you really want an active fund despite the prospect of underperformance, on average, then you should look elsewhere.

So we have one more problem for expensive active funds. Academics have found that performance has on average been poor in multiple prior studies, but now it appears that a reasonable proportion of them have been investing as overpriced index trackers all along.

In addition to paying for an active fund and getting something that tracks the index more than you expect, being active also drives up your transaction costs. Smaller funds in particular can have high transaction costs that reduce their returns, since they are able to benefit from economies of scale in their fund operations. However, this is a double-edged sword. Sometimes smaller funds can do slightly better in picking stocks due to their size, though again these returns generally end up to be negative after fees and transaction costs are factored in. It's little comfort to know that your fund has great stock-picking skills if the result is that the fund ultimately lags the market they are trying to beat.

The Other Costs of Active Management

Being an active investor also brings other direct costs. It bears repeating that in taxable accounts, the costs of short-term trading are high because, generally, any gain held for less than a year is taxed at a higher tax rate than a gain held for a longer period. The impact of that on your returns can be far more than a lot of people realize, especially since it doesn't show up on a stock chart.

The second cost is simply the cost of trading itself. There are multiple elements here, and they do add up. Obviously, the commission is the cost many focus on, and for smaller trades, that can be a material factor. It's often a good reason to use an ETF to acquire many stocks at once rather than attempting to build a portfolio individually. However, the bid-ask spread can erode your returns, especially when you are trading in larger quantities. The bid-ask spread is the difference between the price at which you can buy and the price at which you can sell. Even though the market tracks the "mid" price (the average of the bid and the ask), the investor typically doesn't get that price. The result is that you pay a cost every time you trade, even if it's commission free, and for smaller or less liquid investments bid-ask spreads can be very significant. Obviously, these costs are proportional to how much you trade, so it's one more reason to trade less. The final issue is market impact. As an individual investor, you may not believe you can move the market, but it's certainly possible that your actions impact the price of the security you are trading, just as occurs with every market participant, so your decision to buy may slightly push up the price of a stock just as your decision to sell may slightly reduce it. Again, it's a cost of trading, and the less you trade, the less it eats into your portfolio.

There is one final issue to consider with mutual funds. It is surprisingly hard to align incentives between the fund managers and the investors. Investors are generally unable to determine whether the fund manager is working in their best interests because they are not expert in investing. They cannot assess whether too much risk is being taken and whether apparently good results are due to real investment skill, temporary luck, or, even worse, fraud. Simply paying a manager more for good results doesn't solve the problem because it may also lead the manager to take on more risk, and again good results don't always mean the manager is doing a good job—they might just be lucky.

One example of how this problem could manifest is investors' desire to maximize risk-adjusted returns versus a fund manager's desire to maximize fund inflows. Research by Chevalier and Ellison has shown that funds that are performing well do in fact take risk off the table in the final months of the year.[3] This implies that there is a desire to lock in a good performance number when returns are looking good through most of the year, rather than pursue a constant strategy. This is not necessarily in the interest of investors, since it may involve a fund deviating from a strategy that's working and cause additional turnover, but may help fund inflows by attempting to lock in good performance for year-end.

So the message is clear. The less you trade, the more of your money you get to keep. This is just as true for your individual trades as it is for a mutual fund or ETF. But also remember that if you do chose an active mutual fund, and by this point I really hope you don't give all the evidence that they underperform, bear in mind that much of their portfolio is likely to be tracking the market, so you are paying perhaps more than you think for that portion of the portfolio that truly deviates from a passive fund.

KEY TAKEAWAYS

- Many active funds actually track benchmarks to a much greater extent than you may expect.
- This means that you are paying a premium for the portion of the fund that is active.
- Funds may also revert to tracking the benchmark to lock in periods of good performance, but this may not be what investors expect.

Notes

1. Antti Petajisto, "Active Share and Mutual Fund Performance." *Financial Analysts Journal* 69(4) (2013): 73–93.
2. Martijn Cremers and Antti Petajisto, "How Active Is Your Fund Manager? A New Measure that Predicts Performance KJM Cremers, *Review of Financial Studies* 22(9) (2009): 3329–3365.
3. Judith Chevalier and Glenn Ellison, "Risk Taking by Mutual Funds as a Response to Incentives." *Journal of Political Economy* 105(6) (1997): 1167–1200.

Chapter 13

The Greatest Mistakes Made by Novice Investors

"The investor's chief problem—even his worst enemy—is likely to be himself."

—Benjamin Graham

S ome of the biggest mistakes made by novice investors stem from the fact that the value of the Standard & Poor's (S&P) 500 is one of the most widely reported numbers by the media. This focuses attention on pretax returns within the United States. There are two problems with that. The first is that tax is a big deal in investing and something you can control fairly easily with some simple steps. The second is that the focus on the U.S. market means that many investors are not as diversified as they should be. Here are some quick tips to make sure that your portfolio doesn't have any major flaws.

Starting Saving Too Late

One of the most important numbers for your investment strategy is your savings rate. As discussed in Chapter 1, that number is too low for many American households. However, starting saving as soon as you can is critically important, too. Not only does it increase the amount of your savings, but it also gives your money more time to grow due to the logic of compounding—it helps your money make money. Digital advisors are helpful in this regard, in that you are able to start saving with low minimums, typically just several thousand dollars, so there's no barrier to getting started for most people.

Not Starting Early Enough

"You talk about the dot com crash like you were there."

Source: Huw Aaron

Are You Using Tax Shelters Effectively?

If you have a particular savings goal in mind, whether college, retirement, or a first home, the IRS offers various savings vehicles to help you save for that goal and defer or eliminate taxes. Using these tax shelters effectively can help your money grow much faster than if it were in a taxable account, and the benefit increases if you are in a high-tax bracket or live in a high-tax state.

Are You Taking Advantage of 401(k) Matching If Available?

According to a 2012 analysis by Brightscope, 47 percent of company retirement plans offer some form of investment contribution matching. Most commonly, this is contribution match up to a certain level, though tiered matching or fixed cash lump-sum matches are also possible. As an employee, these can be an attractive benefit, assuming you already need to save for retirement. Contribution matching offers not only the ability to take advantage of the tax-deferred growth of 401(k) savings but also the opportunity to have up to 100 percent of your contributions matched at the outset. This is almost like a free pay raise at work, and offers a very attractive way to save for retirement. In fact, the gains of participating are so great that it's worth contributing up to the matching level even if fees are relatively high or the contributions relatively limited.

Are You Diversified Internationally?

As discussed in Chapter 8, home bias is common in many countries of the world, including the United States. The temptation to hold what you know, whether the big companies in your own state, stock in your employer, or companies in your own country, is common. However, this leads to a poorly constructed portfolio. International diversification can reduce risk and potentially level returns over time. In addition, this diversification can improve your sector exposure because sectors are not evenly distributed between countries, and some countries have a bias toward particular industries. Holding a broad cross-section of industries also helps your portfolio and is relatively simple to do by diversifying internationally.

Are You Chasing Returns?

Research by DALBAR has shown that timing is one of an investor's biggest enemies. Fear of missing out can make it easy to chase a rising market and buy something that may be getting expensive. Equally, it can be hard to hold on to an investment that's losing money, even though the decline in price may make the prospect of better returns in the future greater. In fact, unfortunately, an investor's timing is generally okay during mild markets; it's during the extreme highs and lows when the big errors occur. Of course, this is not to say that market timing is easy. The message is that buy-and-hold is a robust strategy. It takes away the need for trading decisions beyond rebalancing rules, which an algorithm can implement on your behalf with precision. This is desirable, because often rebalancing means buying something when it has fallen and selling what may be becoming expensive. This can be emotionally difficult to do, but computers can implement such strategies meticulously.

Source: Huw Aaron

Are You Overpaying in Fees?

As described in Chapter 10 on the triumph of low-cost investing, there are multiple studies that have found that lower fee funds generally outperform their more expensive equivalents, and that even if a fund has a history of good performance, this has no predictive value for future returns. Sometimes higher fees are spent, in part, on marketing budgets, so there's no shortage of persuasive messages encouraging you to pay up for high-fee investments, but the studies consistently show that, on average, they fail to deliver.

Are You Tracking the Right Index?

Some indexes are better than others. For example the Dow Jones is not a particularly good index for the buy-and-hold investor. Admittedly, the Dow was one of the first indexes out there. But just as no one criticized the Wright Brothers for not offering Wi-Fi on the first flight, so Dow's innovation in summarizing the stock market in a single number was a smart move. In fact, the Wright Brothers and Charles Dow and Edward Jones came up with their new ideas within a decade of each other. One of these innovations is now confined to museums; the other lives on in daily financial updates.

The Dow Jones Industrial Index now appears outdated and doesn't merit its place alongside other, more modern and better-constructed investing benchmarks. A succession of more advanced aircraft have replaced the Wright Brothers' flyer as a means of air travel, and yet the Dow Jones Industrial Index is still a prominent part of financial summaries the world over. It also happens that the Dow is a fairly expensive index to track with exchange-traded funds (ETFs). There are other ETFs available that track 100 times the companies for just a quarter of the cost.

In the past decades since the forming of the Dow Jones index, more and better indices have been founded. In fact, Dow Jones themselves now offer many better indices than the Dow Jones Industrial Average. The Dow's advantage is its iconic status. However, there are vastly better things to use for both investing and benchmarking.

There are several issues with the Dow. Most important is that it's a poorly diversified benchmark, even though it expanded from 10 stocks when it first launched to 30 stocks in 1928. Historical analysis suggests that holding at a minimum of 100 stocks is helpful to better diversify a portfolio. Even then, counting the number of stocks is a crude measure of diversification. If you held stocks in 100 different U.S. regional banks, you wouldn't be diversified. The Dow has the following selection criteria that their committee considers for periodic adjustments:

> A stock typically is added to The Dow® only if the company has an excellent reputation, demonstrates sustained growth and is of interest to a large number of investors. Maintaining adequate sector representation within the indices is also a consideration in the selection process.

Only the final point here is likely to help diversification; the others mean that the Dow is composed of larger U.S. companies. That selection bias can hurt returns. Studies suggest that over the longer term, having a bias to owning smaller and cheaper companies rather than larger and expensive ones can improve absolute performance. So not only is the Dow too small in terms of its membership, but it also may be using the wrong criteria from an investment return standpoint.

The Dow's constituents are weighted based on price. Again, when it was one of the first indices, these seemed, understandably, the easiest way to implement things. Now, weighting components based on price is actually pretty medieval compared to how advanced the rest of finance is. Goldman Sachs is currently the largest component of the index. Why? Because its stock, at the time of writing, trades around $200. Next up is IBM, with a price closer to $150, and so forth. Microsoft trades at less than $50 and so gets a smaller weight despite being more than three times the size of Goldman Sachs by market cap.

Price weighting is a curious thing. What do you think should happen to the Dow, given current prices, if GE had an incredibly bad day and fell 30 percent and on that same day Goldman Sachs stock rose 5 percent, and all the other Dow components stayed flat? Surprisingly, because Goldman has a higher stock price than GE, the Dow would actually rise for the day in this scenario. That's true even though Goldman is a much smaller company by market cap than GE, about a third the size. Of course, these examples are theoretical, but you can see that as a barometer of the financial markets, there are much better processes for constructing indices.

Because of its small membership and large-cap focus, the Dow Jones also has more turnover than it needs to, which is generally bad for investors because of the costs associated with trading and the tax consequences. A handful of stocks enter and leave the Dow Jones every one to three years. But when you only have 30 constituents, changing just 3 stocks can easily mean 10 percent turnover, especially when compared to a more efficient model where you track hundreds or thousands of stocks. With more stocks and looser criteria, the need to enter and leave is less likely, and even if they did due to an initial public offering or a delisting, any given stock would be a much smaller proportion of the index. If stocks you are holding are more stable over time, then for most investors that's going to be cheaper from a trading cost standpoint, and potentially more tax efficient.

The Dow also highlights the problem of home bias in investing. Globally, investors tend to hold the vast majority of the assets in their portfolio in assets within their home country. Investors have become more global in past decades, but the fundamental bias remains. That's generally not a great move. Investing globally can smooth and sometimes even increase returns depending on where you're starting from. Yet having such a prominent index include only U.S. stocks is old-fashioned. Of course, you can argue that stocks such as Apple are international and that's true to some extent, but there is still a U.S. bias in where they make their profits. Overall, the evidence is persuasive that international investing is a better course, and yet indices such as the Dow prompt people to think only domestically when it comes to investing.

Do You Trade Too Much?

Trading comes with its own costs. Of course, there's the direct cost in commissions, but also the bid-ask spread, any market impact of the trade, and also tax considerations, especially if you're holding investments for under a year in taxable accounts. Couple that with the challenge of successful stock picking and the broad availability of ETFs that can track well-constructed indices that hold an evolving basket of stocks and it makes sense to use ETFs and hold them for the long term, rather than pick stocks that can reduce your diversification and increase your trading costs.

Source: Huw Aaron

KEY TAKEAWAYS

- Investing mistakes can stem from doing too much; often, doing less can achieve more.
- Tax efficient investing is a relatively low-risk way to boost returns.
- Diversification and sticking to a strategy are helpful tactics.
- Chasing past returns seldom helps a portfolio.

Chapter 14

Tilts and Other Ways to Help Long-Term Performance

"Spend each day trying to be a little wiser than you were when you woke up."

—Charlie Munger

The stock market is broadly efficient. This means that is not easy to outperform the broader stock market over time after all costs are factored in. Of course, let's remember that this doesn't necessarily make the stock market a bad investment. Being average is okay, since historically even average returns have been good. Just by tracking the index many investors have done well, but it does mean that beating the index is a challenge.

Table 14.1   Assessing Portfolio Tilts—A 2 × 2 Matrix

	High Implementation Cost	Low Implementation Cost
Data-Backed Tilt	Your broker makes money, but you don't *Example: Momentum trading by buying and selling 100s of stocks with retail commissions in a taxable account and changing the set of investments each month*	Robust long-term strategy *Example: Value tilt via low-cost ETF*
Spurious Tilt	Large performance drag *Example: Believing you can profitably create short-term option strategies based on the CEO's haircut*	Slight performance drag *Example: Overweighting midcap stocks through an ETF*

Source: FutureAdvisor Analysis

However, several strategies beyond basic index investing have been shown to contribute to performance history. Unfortunately, there is no free lunch.

Often, these strategies require a long-term investment horizon and entail greater tax inefficiency or other costs. Sometimes the cost is more in terms of behavioral rigor needed to implement the strategy effectively. Certain strategies are simply hard to follow or have the potential to make you look stupid if they fail, which can particularly be an issue for professional money managers who report actions to their clients periodically. So the question is not does the strategy work but does the strategy work predictably after all costs, including behavioral costs are factored in? Performing this analysis leads to a narrower set of feasible options. Table 14.1 shows this. Ideal strategies both have underlying performance value, but also enhance returns after all costs are factored in. Unfortunately, there are many strategies that work in principle, but once all implementation costs are considered, then the value of the strategy becomes negative.

History of Market Thought

In the 1970s the idea of strong-form market efficiency was widespread. Academics wrote broadly on how markets were sufficiently efficient to be basically random. Eugene Fama of the University of Chicago provided a summary in a 1973 article in the *Journal of Finance*. He stated, "Evidence in support of efficient markets is extensive, and (somewhat unique in economics) contradictory evidence is sparse."[1]

However, Fama did make the important caveat that "we do not want to leave the impression that all issues are closed." At the time, many studies had focused on short-term market efficiency looking at how prices change in the weeks after important events. Generally, prices were shown to be random.

However, subsequently analysis of price movements over longer-term months and years has shown that some patterns exist—patterns that should be impossible if markets were truly efficient. Indeed, some of these trends were demonstrated in later research by Eugene Fama himself, the very researcher who had summarized market efficiency in the first place.

There were two other contradictions to efficient markets.

Over the 1980s several papers emerged showing that the markets moved up and down more than basic models suggested they should. Robert Shiller, who subsequently won the Nobel Prize, argued that prices moved up and down by double to quadruple what you might expect.[2] This insight lead to the Shiller cyclically adjusted price-to-earnings ratio, showing that stock prices were at least somewhat forecastable and again modifying the idea that markets were simply random.

Then, in the 1990s, behavioral economics emerged as a discipline related to psychology showing that people didn't always make rational economic decisions. Gains and losses were not treated in the same way, and reaction to recent events was greater than rationality suggested.

As a result, the idea of market efficiency has been modified somewhat to the point where markets are believed to almost impossible to forecast over periods of days or months, but over longer time periods market returns can be partially projected, in part because markets sometimes overreact more than rational models suggest they should; in part because humans and therefore investors are not as rational as the economic models that predict their behavior; and in part because certain tilts to portfolios may offer the prospect of better performance. Market efficiency nonetheless remains a good starting point and indeed a better one with which investors can make easy money than with naive predictions, but there are clear weaknesses in the strongest form of market efficiency.

Data Mining

There is also risk of data mining with these strategies. Many researchers and practitioners are looking for these opportunities in the market. With decades of data and thousands of stocks, and now with tremendous computing power at our disposal, there is a risk of finding anomalies that are accidents in a sea of data rather than something with real predictive power. For example, you might find that the price of cod in Iceland serves as a leading indicator of the Standard & Poor's (S&P) 500, but this is just a random occurrence with so much data out there it may be possible to "see" a statistical relationship where no predictive power exists. Correlation is not causation. However, this problem can be overcome in several ways. One of the more powerful strategies is to look across time periods and markets; if an effect exists in multiple countries over multiple time periods, then it may have greater validity. The second important area to note is the existence of a credible hypothesis to explain the phenomenon. We have to be careful here when following scientific process. Strictly speaking, the hypothesis should come before testing the data, rather than after. Nonetheless, if there is a credible logic behind the statistical phenomenon, then it is less likely to be a fluke. Third, it's important to consider statistical testing, statistics can measure how likely something is to occur randomly, and if the chances are smaller, then we can be somewhat more confident of something real. Fourth, the real test is out-of-sample performance. How has a particular strategy done after it has been discovered? Even this data isn't clear-cut, unfortunately; the fact that something has persisted out of sample doesn't mean it can't end at any point in the future. A final consideration is implementation consistency. Even the best strategies can offer low incremental improvements to returns of 1 percent to 2 percent before costs in most cases. It's tempting to implement multiple strategies, but some are contradictory and cannot necessarily be combined. So a final layer of analysis must be performed when looking at multiple strategies to make sure that one will not offset or counteract the other.

However, if a strategy can pass the following tests, then it may be valid:

- Has it worked across time periods?
- Has it worked across geographies?
- Is there a valid reason to explain why this effect occurs?

- Is it able to provide a positive return after taking account of all costs including taxation and turnover?
- Will implementing the strategy cause any behavioral issues/risks?
- Can it be combined with other strategies already being implemented?

Debunking Strong-Form Market Efficiency

The other concern with these effects is the broader concern that if markets are efficient, then this whole enterprise is pointless. By definition these effects cannot exist. Wall Street contains many smart teams of people and trading algorithms, so beating the pooled intelligence of the market is going to be a lofty goal. Second, for every buyer there is a seller, so any effect cannot work at scale. Everyone, in aggregate, must earn the market's return less costs.

The first point suggests that effects are hard to find but also gives an insight into why the markets are reasonably efficient. It is because many smart people work to find opportunities, exploit them, and receive a slightly higher return for doing so. The Nobel Prize–winning economist Milton Friedman was a proponent of this view. The result of this activity is to push the market closer to a "fair" value over time. Any market participant who does analysis gets, on average, some level of compensation for doing so. Now, they may not end up ahead after costs, but it's possible they see some incremental performance boost for their efforts.

Second, it's true that in aggregate everything is a wash, so if everyone implemented these strategies, they would either cease to exist or become counterproductive. However, crucially, not everyone has the investment goals or the temperament to accommodate these strategies. Over time, their impact may erode, but the fact that they can't exist if everyone implements them doesn't mean they don't exist, because not everyone implements them.

Rationality

It's also worth considering the enormous impact behavioral finance has had in past decades. People make mistakes all the time, often in predictable ways. People generally worry far more about air travel than road travel, even though driving is far riskier on a per-mile basis. We care more about avoiding losses than achieving gains. We remember things that are more vivid and recent, at the expense of things that might be more likely to happen in future. There is an assumption that these biases should end when people start investing for big stakes, but research has shown they may not. This is another reason to believe in market anomalies, especially when they play into known flaws in human decision making. Behavioral financial is a field with increasing credibility and influence and now has a Nobel Prize to show for it.

The January Effect

The January effect argues for purchasing value stocks in January. Typically, the stock market does well in January and those stocks that have performed poorly over the past year can do particularly well during the month. This effect has been rationalized due to tax-loss selling. In the United States and other regions, investors can benefit from incurring losses, rather than just having a paper loss in their portfolio because the loss offers some tax benefit. Typically, investors tend to take stock of these opportunities before the tax year ends. In addition, professional investors often have to declare their holdings to clients on a quarterly basis, and window dressing is possible. A professional investor doesn't want to show that they have held a dud stock over the course of the year, so they sell it before it appears in the report to clients. These effects may both serve to push down the effect of poor-performing stocks at the end of the calendar year, only for investors wanting to buy them back in January given that this year may be better than the last. Of course, this effect is not a free lunch. By definition it involves a relatively short holding period, which is inefficient for the majority of investors. It also involves buying stocks that have fallen in value, often significantly. This is behaviorally hard to do. Finally, though the strategy may work in aggregate, it can lead to losses in certain cases, relative to other strategies. Again, this creates a barrier to implementation.

Sell in May and Go Away

In some sense, selling in May and repurchasing stocks in the late summer is a sibling of the January effect. The January effect boosts returns over the winter, and summer returns have been shown to lag. This effect is harder to rationalize; perhaps the early optimistic projections at the start of the year meet with a more hard-nosed analysis over the summer months, but it's unclear. Equally, the power of this one is less clear-cut. Returns may lag over the summer, but not necessarily in a way that creates a trading opportunity. As with the January effect, there's some tax inefficiency from having a holding period of less than a year and the markets still rise over the summer, just by less than average, so it's unclear how to trade this profitably.

Momentum

Jegadeesh and Titman published the seminal research on this topic in 1993,[3] and the academic evidence has been getting stronger since then. Basically, stocks that have risen in value relative to the market over periods of less than a year tend to show better-than-average returns. The exact implementation can vary from picking the best 3- to 12-month performers and holding them for another 3 to 12 months. It's a counterintuitive strategy; often, people like to sell winners and lock in gains, as all-time highs suggest that a return to normal might be around the corner rather than further gains. Again, it's a relatively costly and tax-inefficient strategy. By definition you are holding investments for under a year so the tax and trading costs can add up, creating a cost hurdle to be overcome relative to buy-and-hold. Second, the strategy can add risk. It works overall, but if you happen to be implementing a momentum strategy at a time of market decline, then your returns can be weaker than average. This is a problem, of course, because there's no good time to lose money, but underperforming a weak market can be especially hard. These are the times where you are more likely to lose your job or your clients, so everyone is more sensitive to risk in these environments. Nonetheless, the academic evidence for momentum suggests that it works over time so far.

Value

Value is a classic strategy, as first emphasized by Fama and French in their 1992 paper.[4] This was particularly interesting because two researchers who were passionate advocates of the efficient market model wrote a paper finding a key weakness—certainly not a killer blow to efficient markets, but definitely a loosening of the thinking.

Value strategies employ a bias to stocks that are "cheap" on some metric in terms of having more assets, earnings or cash flow per your dollar of investment average. Of course, what you might expect is that these stocks are cheap for a reason—poor growth or the prospect of bankruptcy means that the value is an illusion. However, what researchers found is that the value effect comes out ahead. Those stocks that appear to be cheap actually are slightly cheaper in aggregate, and those more expensive stocks that are believed to have better prospects actually don't turn out to be so superior in terms of their long term performance.

This is a strategy that can be behaviorally hard to implement. You're buying stocks that aren't making the headlines for innovation or growth. They aren't the darlings of the media, and past performance often has been rocky. Also, it's not a consistent strategy—you may make money over time but not steadily every month or every year.

Interestingly, in a recent refinement to their initial model moving to five factors from three, Fama and French find that the value effect can disappear when firm profitability and level of balance sheet growth are reflected as variables. However, given that these tilts are not currently implementable at low cost, value appears a preferable cost-benefit trade-off for investors.[5]

Small Cap

Smaller stocks tend to outperform larger ones. This one is not too stable and can persist for many years only to fail for a string of years. However, it can improve returns. It works particularly well for very small stocks, and some have argued that trading costs are larger for these stocks, and also delisting of these stocks is more prevalent than average so the effect may be overstated.

Quality

Quality is relatively newer and finds that stocks that appear more robust with greater profit margins, without excessive debt, and more stable positions do better over time. Research deconstructing the performance of Warren Buffett's portfolio has shown quality to be a significant element in how Buffett picks investments.[6]

Longer-Term Mean Reversion

This effect suggest that over time stocks come back to average, broadly speaking, over a three- to five-year period the winners tend to underperform the market and the losers start to show some gains. It's the opposite of momentum but is consistent with it because the time period is different. Momentum works in the short term, but in the long term, reversion to the mean tends to occur. This is a strategy that can be cheap to implement because the holding period can be relatively long, and it can be done in a tax-efficient way. However, it can be behaviorally challenging to buy the worst-performing stocks and see some of them do even worse after you buy them, even if things do work out eventually. De Bondt and Thaler are the main practitioners behind this concept from their 1985 paper.[7]

Assessing Tilts in a Portfolio Context

Looking at tilts on a stand-alone basis, even if we have conviction that they are not historical accidents and may persist, is not enough. We need to have conviction that we can implement the strategy to earn a better return on the portfolio after the impact of all costs and taxes relative to a basic buy-and-hold portfolio without any tilts to it. For example, the need to sell an investment within a year, due to a particular strategy, can often impact the returns to a strategy because it can create short-term capital gains. Another risk is that exchange-traded funds (ETFs) that implement the strategy might charge too high an expense ratio to make the strategy profitable. That is to say, there are gains to be had, but the higher fees of implementation eat all the gains so the investor doesn't get any.

KEY TAKEAWAYS

- There are various ways to attempt to outperform the market, but many fail once the full implementation and immediate tax costs of the strategies are considered.
- Value and small-cap biases are two tilts that can be implemented in a low-cost manner using ETFs.
- As the costs of ETFs decline, further strategies may become profitable for investors.

Notes

1. John T. Emery. "Efficient Capital Markets and the Information Content of Accounting Numbers." *The Journal of Financial and Quantitative Analysis* 9(02) (1974):139–149.
2. John Y. Campbell and Robert J. Shiller, "Stock Prices, Earnings, and Expected Dividends." *The Journal of Finance* 43(3) (1988): 661–676.
3. Narasimhan Jegadeesh and Sheridan Titman, "Returns to Buying Winners and Selling Losers: Implications for Stock Market Efficiency." *The Journal of Finance* 48(1) (1993): 65–91.
4. Eugene F. Fama and Kenneth R. French, "The Cross-Section of Expected Stock Returns." *The Journal of Finance* 47(2) (1992): 427–465.
5. Eugene F. Fama and Kenneth R. French, "A Five-Factor Asset Pricing Model." *Journal of Financial Economics* 116(1) (2015): 1–22.
6. Andrea Frazzini, David Kabiller, and Lasse H. Pedersen, "Buffett's Alpha." Yale Department of Economics, August 2012.
7. Werner F. M. De Bondt and Richard Thaler, "Does the Stock Market Overreact?" *The Journal of Finance* 40(3) (1985): 793–805.

Chapter 15

Establishing a Tax-Efficient Portfolio

"The hardest thing to understand in the world is the income tax."
—Albert Einstein

B eing smart about tax can be your secret weapon in building a strong portfolio. As with other forms of income, the government takes a share of the money you make on your investments. This means that the returns you see on paper typically don't translate to the returns you actually make after taxes are accounted for.

What if there was a way to boost your returns by 20 percent a year? Wait you say, the markets are pretty efficient, so a simple way to edge up returns by 20 percent a year can't exist. Once tax comes into play there is some easy money to be had and it's perfectly legal. Usage of tax shelters, avoiding short-term capital gains, tax loss harvesting, and tax-efficient asset placement have the potential to materially improve post-tax returns.

In fact, the government wants to encourage you to be a long-term saver especially for savings goals like retirement or education. Of course, the government gets less in tax in the short run, but if retirees are financially secure and people are well educated, then society benefits in the long run. So the tax strategies we describe here are not an attempt to avoid taxes, but to set up your investments in a way that's supported by the current tax system and purposefully plans for important life events from your own retirement to a child's or grandchild's retirement.

The basic challenge with tax is that it's not an enticing thing to learn about so many people don't. That's an understandable but expensive mistake. Fortunately, whereas people find tax boring, algorithms are well suited to it. This chapter will walk through the tax areas that will materially help your savings performance. One of the biggest ones is taking advantage of tax shelters. Most investments are taxed each year on investment gains. However, certain accounts are not. This is very helpful to returns, because deferring tax means you can earn money on that money and often tax can be deferred for decades. Your saving for retirement, then—a 401(k), 457(b), 403(b), or individual retirement account (IRA) will defer tax and possibly eliminate it altogether. Equally, if you're saving for college, then a 529 or Coverdell can achieve the same thing.

Of course, there is a trade-off with these tax shelters. They are all linked to a particular goal, so penalties come into play if you don't use the funds for that particular purpose. If you don't use 529 funds for college or an IRA for retirement, then penalties will typically offset the benefits, but if you can plan ahead with your savings, then you'll likely see a benefit in how fast your money grows.

Eliminating or defer the taxes you pay by using these tax shelters, gives a real boost to your savings. You can further benefit from this by having a tax-efficient allocation within your portfolio, this means being selective about what sort of investments go in your taxable and nontaxable accounts.

Finally, within your taxable account, tax loss harvesting can defer taxes into the future, which again helps performance, because you earn a return on the money that would have been paid in taxes. Again, fortunately, algorithms are set up to help here. Tax efficiency is a rules-based and repetitive process, perfectly suited to implementation in software.

A tax-efficient portfolio is something of an unsung hero in investing. Stock pickers and pundits, often with dubious long-term records get a lot of credit on Wall Street, but you seldom hear about someone doing a great job on tax efficiency. However, the gains from tax efficiency can easily rival those of even expert stock pickers. More importantly, tax efficiency is a lot easier, less time consuming and generally far less risky. This chapter is focused on showing you how to do it. In particular, you'll see that tax loss harvesting is best done algorithmically.

Tax Shelters

The first thing to focus on is efficient use of tax-sheltered account. A tax-sheltered account typically has a specific savings goal in mind. There can be a little flexibility in use at the margin, but often there is a cash penalty if you don't use it for the goal for which it's intended, and if you end up paying those penalties, you're no better off than if you'd use a normal taxable account for those savings. The main focus of these tax-sheltered savings products is retirement and college savings.

Tax Efficiency for Retirement

The government has a range of vehicle to help you save for retirement at a lower tax rate than you'd otherwise pay. A common tool is 401(k)s, where your employer sets up a set of choices to get you on track for retirement, and often provides contribution matching to encourage you to save. If you work in certain sectors of the economy you may have options beyond a 401(k). 403(b) plans generally serve nonprofits and 457 plans are generally used for government employees. Both have similar function to a 401(k), though 457 plans generally have lower penalties for withdrawal of the funds before retirement. 401(k) contributions can be tax free and grow without being taxed; through withdrawals, money will likely be taxed as income in retirement. Traditional IRAs have a similar structure, though income limits mean that higher earners may not qualify. Roth IRAs have a different structure, where tax is paid on contributions, but the money is never taxed again. If you are in a low tax rate at the moment, but expect to be in a higher one in the future, then a Roth IRA can be a great savings tool. If you're self-employed or working for a small business, there is a range of savings options for retirement that are generally simpler to administer than 401(k) plans but, again, with a similar tax structure.

As great as 401(k) plans are from a tax standpoint—and often match-ing benefits from your employer are about as close as you get to free money—there is one major limitation in that the choices your employer offers you may not be that enticing. This is not a reason not to use them because the tax and potential matching benefits will generally offset the implicit costs of a limited range of options, but there are a few things to watch out for. The first is to avoid employer stock where you can. Em-ployers have been able to include their own stock as a 401(k) option for some time. Generally, it's a poor choice from a portfolio standpoint. You already have a lot riding on your employer. You may not see it in your stock portfolio, but a large proportion of your future assets will come from your paycheck, any bonuses or pay raises you may get in the future, and career advancement opportunities. Now, all of these to a greater or lesser degree are dependent on the financial health of your employer. Hence, you already have a relatively significant financial bet on your employer. If your employer were to experience financial problems, then you may need to find other employment or at least see your paycheck grow slower than it otherwise would. You don't want to add stock own-ership in your employer to that mix. Then, in the bad scenario, you'd see everything decline at once—your current earnings and your savings. There's no need to take that risk. In fact, it's also worth avoiding invest-ing in companies that are too similar to your employer. If you work for a bank, then investing in bank stocks generally probably isn't a good idea from a risk standpoint.

Tax Efficiency for College

Saving for college has several options. A 529 plan enables your money to grow tax free, and it won't be taxed when it's taken out to pay for college for the recipient. A Coverdell education savings account (ESA) has a similar structure but can be used for a broader range of educa-tional costs beyond college, including K–12 costs. However, Coverdell ESAs have income contribution limits and relatively low contribution limits, so if you're a high earner or a big saver, you may not be eligible or use it up relatively fast. Finally, trusts also present an option for col-lege savings. These can be a useful way to manage estate planning and potentially reduce inheritance taxes and are extremely flexible in terms

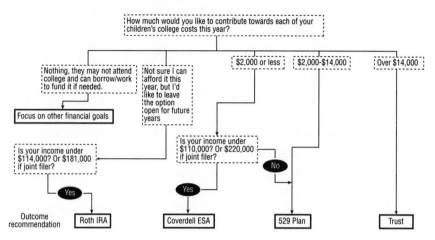

Figure 15.1 College Savings Flowchart

of how the money is invested and used. However, the tax benefits are more limited, and the child will pay tax on the income, which typically isn't an issue, beyond some paperwork, when the earnings are limited, but if the account is substantial or the child is earning money himself, then the earnings may be taxed at a rate similar to the rate on your own account. Also, most legal trust structures mean that the money transfers to the child at 18 or 21, so potentially the child could choose to use the money in a way that you as the parent may not agree with, rather than spend it on education.

The flowchart in Figure 15.1 helps you work through appropriate college savings options.

Once your tax shelters are set up, the next step is to use them appropriately.

Tax Efficiency for Giving

You have an opportunity to help your portfolio when you give to a charity. Many nonprofits can receive stock, rather than cash, as a contribution. However, any capital gains at the time the stock is given will not be paid by you or the nonprofit. This means that if you're planning a gift to charity, then giving appreciated stock from your taxable portfolio may be a smart way to do it.

Tax-Efficient Asset Placement

If you're like most investors, it's probable you'll have multiple accounts either because you have different savings goals and different accounts for each or because you max out a contribution level in a particular year and use a taxable account for the remainder of your savings.

Being smart about which investments you place where can be a helpful tax strategy. This doesn't mean altering the composition of your portfolio necessarily. At FutureAdvisor we calculate optimal portfolios for clients *before* the decision to place assets in specific portfolios. This is because the best portfolio for you is a reflection of your risk tolerance and time period over which you expect to be saving, among other factors. Aiming to buy investments simply because they are tax efficient is backwards; a sensible portfolio structure should come first. Tax is an important consideration, but if you construct your portfolio solely for tax reasons, then the tail is wagging the dog.

Some assets result in greater taxation than others, particularly when a buy-and-hold strategy is used. The obvious example is real estate investment trusts (REITs). Created by Congress in 1960, REITs enable liquid investment in real estate, but REITs are required to pay out at least 90 percent of taxable income as dividends to investors. Many other stocks don't pay dividends at all, or pay out much less than 90 percent of taxable income. As an investor, you typically pay tax on dividends in the tax year you receive them. Therefore, you should consider placing REITs within a tax-sheltered account such as a 401(k), IRA, or similar account. It's likely they'll generate more income than most other assets under a buy-and-hold strategy because of the large dividend payout. At the time of writing, the yield on REITs is about double that of most equity indices and higher than on most diversified bond funds. As an investor, if you can defer taxation on those dividends, your money will grow faster.

After REITs, the relative growth and income of investments and their tax efficiency should be considered, as well as the space available in tax-sheltered accounts. Fixed-income instruments can make sense to be sheltered as the asset class due to their relatively high taxable income. Furthermore, having equities in taxable accounts can be useful for tax loss harvesting, as typically they are more volatile than fixed income.

For example, the Standard & Poor's (S&P) 500 as a typical stock market benchmark has historically returned over 50 percent in very good years, but also lost more than 50 percent in certain years. Fixed income tends to be more stable; returns of 10 percent and losses of 10 percent are both relatively extreme events in the history of U.S. Treasury bonds, for example. The relatively higher volatility of equities is another reason to consider them for taxable accounts, since tax loss harvesting is not possible in a tax-sheltered account because no tax is paid.

The final step is being smart about tax in your taxable account, and that's where tax loss harvesting comes in.

Tax Loss Harvesting

Tax loss harvesting can be a valuable strategy to boost after-tax returns in taxable accounts. Taxes can erode the value of a portfolio so that actual returns are significantly lower than market returns. This is true even for an investor able to track the market's returns perfectly. This can impact all investors, but especially impacts those in higher tax brackets. Over time, taxes can be a material expense for investors and meaningfully reduce retirement savings.

Offsetting Gains with Losses

Tax loss harvesting enables an investor to eliminate or offset capital gains with capital losses. Tax loss harvesting has been a regular component of wealthier investors' strategies for some time; more recently, however, algorithmic investing has made it possible to implement the strategy even across small accounts. Tax loss harvesting does not require an active investment style or frequent trading. It can be valuable even to an investor pursuing a fundamental buy-and-hold strategy, with periodic rebalancing, such as with FutureAdvisor's Premium product. Under tax loss harvesting, while losses are realized to provide tax benefits, the portfolio itself remains similarly invested by holding equivalent positions in similar but alternative securities. As such, if implemented correctly, tax loss harvesting does not necessarily materially impact a portfolio's tracking error; it simply increases tax efficiency. The flow chart in Figure 15.2 shows how tax loss harvesting works.

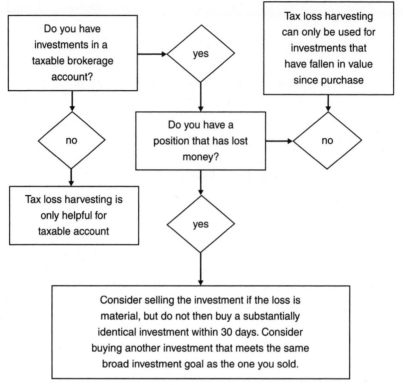

Figure 15.2   Tax Loss Harvesting Flowchart

The Principal of Tax Deferral

For most investors, tax loss harvesting is a process of deferring taxes until a future date. Both the time value of money and inflation prove that paying for something later is preferable to paying sooner. Tax loss harvesting is somewhat like receiving a loan from the IRS, on which you earn money over time. In addition, many people will see their tax bracket fall once in retirement and drawing down on savings; in this scenario, tax loss harvesting may also reduce the tax burden in absolute terms, in addition to the inflation benefit.

Table 15.1 shows the value of deferring $10,000 taxes with 6 percent market returns.

Table 15.1   The Value of Tax Deferral

Years Over Which Taxes Deferred	Increase in Portfolio Value
1	$600
5	$3,382
10	$7,908
20	$22,071

How Tax Loss Harvesting Works

The easiest way to understand the technique's basic principle is to look at a simple example.

Let's say your portfolio consists of $50,000 invested in exchange-traded fund (ETF) X. Then, in a down year, the value of that holding decreases to $45,000. Most investors in this situation would do nothing. An investor implementing tax loss harvesting, however, would sell the $45,000 holding in ETF X and invest it instead in a similar but not substantially identical fund. In doing so, this investor has "harvested" the $5,000 loss for tax purposes, though in reality little actually changed—he or she still owns $45,000 of a mutual fund in that asset class, just as if no action was taken. (Note that the investor must be careful not to buy back ETF X within 31 days, to comply with the IRS's wash sale rule).

Now, because you have booked the $5,000 capital loss, at tax time, you may net this loss against capital gains elsewhere in your portfolio, thereby reducing the amount of capital gains tax you owe in a year when your portfolio earns a net profit. In a year when your capital losses outweigh gains, the IRS allows you to apply up to $3,000 in losses against your other income and to carry over the remaining losses to offset income in future years.

Challenges of Implementing Tax Loss Harvesting

Tax loss harvesting requires diligent tracking of tax lots across a portfolio, as well as monitoring market movements, since opportunities for tax loss harvesting can occur at any time given volatile markets. As such, looking for tax loss harvesting opportunities every few months will be less effective than monitoring for opportunities every day. The value of digital advisory services such as FutureAdvisor is apparent here, given their unique ability to save investors time and effort. An algorithm that can monitor for opportunities whenever markets are open and that understands the optimization process can effectively implement the principles of tax loss harvesting. Note that tax loss harvesting is not relevant for tax-deferred accounts, including IRAs and 401(k)s.

Rules Related to Tax Loss Harvesting

Tax loss harvesting is a technique that wealthy investors frequently use and, if done correctly, is consistent with IRS guidelines and perfectly legal. Two key things to avoid are (1) a "wash sale," in which the same investment is repurchased within 30 days of being sold; and (2) the purchase of an investment that is "substantially identical" to the investment being sold. Either of these errors would invalidate any potential gains from tax loss harvesting.

How Daily Analysis Increases Opportunities for Tax Loss Harvesting Significantly

Analyzing S&P 500 returns from 1950 to the present shows that, assuming one's portfolio is rebalanced or has new money deposited every 60 trading days, the opportunity for tax loss harvesting is far greater with daily analysis. Based on our back-testing, there have been only 15 opportunities for tax loss harvesting since 1950; however, with daily analysis there have been opportunities each year, and often multiple times per year. The broader the interval over which data are analyzed, the more likely the underlying index is to have risen in price. By analyzing data on a more frequent basis, one is more likely to observe price declines (see Table 15.2). This result is a function of the general rise in equity prices historically—the S&P is more likely to decline over a shorter period (a day) than a longer period (a year).

Table 15.2   Frequency of Tax Loss Harvesting Opportunities for S&P 500

Evaluation Frequency	Maximum Potential Opportunities	Number of Tax Loss Opportunities
Daily	16,270	6,586
Weekly	3,373	1,150
Monthly	777	191
Annual	63	15

Source: FutureAdvisor analysis, 1950–present

Other Factors that Impact Tax Loss Harvesting

Though time interval is an important variable, tax loss harvesting is also impacted by the number of assets in the portfolio, with opportunities rising as the number of distinct assets increases. In addition, opportunities are more common in bear markets and for less seasoned portfolios given that prices have historically trended upward for the assets included in FutureAdvisor portfolios.

It is important to consider the impact of taxes in potentially eroding the value of your savings. Tax loss harvesting is a method of tax deferral, which can increase returns. Since algorithms can evaluate opportunities on a daily basis, this method is more beneficial than manual analysis, which is either extremely time consuming, less effective, or both. The gains from effective daily tax loss harvesting can be significant, especially for those with large taxable account balances or in high tax brackets.

Conclusion

Paying attention to your tax situation is one of the best strategies for improving your returns, primarily because if you adhere to IRS rules, many of which are intended to encourage saving, then you can improve your return without increasing portfolio risk. Though you can improve your portfolio in other areas, too, the risk of those changes is highly unlikely to be zero risk, at least over the short term. Also, bear in mind that though tax is a dry topic, it's well suited to algorithms to repeatedly look for opportunities in your portfolio. For example, with tax loss harvesting it's unsurprising that looking daily for opportunities will increase the number of opportunities you see. For a human to do a daily review for opportunities would be mind-numbingly tedious at best, and more than likely expensive, too, but algorithms can perform this task effortlessly.

KEY TAKEAWAYS

- The first step in tax-efficient investing is to use the right accounts. Many accounts can defer or eliminate taxes for certain savings goals. This approach can boost your after-tax returns significantly.
- Your assets should not be mirrored across accounts, but placed in accounts according to their taxable status. For example, REITs, which pay significant dividends, should generally be included in tax-deferred accounts.
- Tax loss harvesting can improve post-tax returns by deferring long-term capital gains without materially changing the investment allocation. Historically, investors have done this process in December of each year, but algorithms can identify these opportunities on an ongoing basis, which can result in 40 percent more opportunities being found.

Chapter 16

The Value of Rebalancing and Glidepaths

"We simply attempt to be fearful when others are greedy and greedy only when others are fearful."

—Warren Buffett

Even within a buy-and-hold portfolio, some degree of rebalancing is necessary. For example, large stock indices such as the Standard & Poor's (S&P) 500 or Dow Jones periodically make decisions about updating membership or weights to certain companies. If this didn't happen, newer companies from Facebook to Apple wouldn't be part of indices, and railroad stocks from the 1880s would presumably dominate the index (back in 1900, railroad companies actually made up more than half of the U.S. stock market). Even over the decade between 1990 and 2000, half of the membership of the S&P 500 changed, and approximately 30 companies join and leave the index each year.[1] Some amount of rebalancing keeps things current. Just as this is valuable within asset classes it is also helpful to portfolios.

Rebalancing Keeps a Portfolio on Course

When a portfolio is created, it has certain characteristics. At a basic level, exposure to stocks that are expected to offer a higher return is balanced by fixed-income exposure, which, in addition to offering a steady return, helps manage risk when stocks perform poorly. Without rebalancing, in a bear market the portfolio may drift to become too conservative relative to its initial goals as stocks decline in value and bonds potentially rise. Conversely, in good markets stock exposure may creep up over time. Neither of these outcomes is good for the investor because the portfolio was created with a certain risk-reward profile in mind, and drifting away from this position because of market movements may lead to a portfolio that does not fit the client's goal. In the case of the stock market falling, the unbalanced portfolio may be unable to capitalize fully on a rebound in stocks as the stock exposure has drifted lower. In the case of the market rising, the portfolio may not offer sufficient downside protection because stock exposure has drifted up, right at the time that stocks have become relatively more expensive.

One example of the value of rebalancing comes from the different behaviors of the California Public Employees' Retirement System (CalPERS) and the Norwegian sovereign wealth fund during 2008–2009, as Andrew Ang documents.[2] During this period, CalPERS lost $70 billion; of course, most lost money during this period. Yet CalPERS made a permanent change to their allocation, prompted in part by unexpected risks in other areas such as real estate. However, Norway's sovereign wealth fund followed investment principles determined by the Norwegian Parliament and were the largest global buyers of equities during the 2008–2009 period, a move that worked out extremely well subsequently. These two examples show the importance of following a disciplined investment strategy, especially because it's the greatest periods of market turmoil that both create the tendency to use the "this time it's different" argument to avoid following predetermined rules and can provide the greatest benefit if rules are appropriately followed.

This example shows why rebalancing matters. It helps align a portfolio with its long-term goals and implicitly counteracts the emotions of fear and greed that can destroy wealth for investors. Therefore, having some rebalancing for a long-term portfolio is useful; otherwise, after a few years, your portfolio will be a combination of accidents resulting from market movements and potentially the occasional trade driven by emotion, rather than the result of a thought-out and comprehensive plan. In financial parlance, your portfolio will have more "tracking error" than you would ideally want. In plain English, your portfolio's performance may be poor.

However, with rebalancing we can also have too much of a good thing. The markets move every day, and trading has explicit costs, implicit costs, and tax consequences to it. Therefore, a trade-off must be found between keeping a portfolio aligned with its client goals and all the costs resulting from frequent trading. For example, even free trades normally incur a bid-ask spread, which eats into your performance every time you trade. It may not surprise you to know that rebalancing is the sort of decision that is well suited to an algorithm, since the opportunity for rebalancing requires diligent and constant monitoring—the sort of thing that would cause a human to make errors but a computer can execute effortlessly. If and when any rebalancing does occur, it should ideally be combined with other portfolio considerations such as tax efficiency, cash and dividend investment, and consideration of whether the initial fund selection is still valid in the presence of current expense ratios, commissions, and bid-ask spreads. Algorithmic decision making can combine these different elements to reach a well-rounded decision for the client portfolio keeping it on track, but not at the expense of introducing other costs that more than offset the benefit.

Rebalancing can be set up to be done every period, such as once a quarter, or on a threshold basis, such as when a bond/equity split deviates more than, say, 2 percent from its target. Time-based rebalancing is shown in Figure 16.1. Each time a time threshold is hit, such as each quarter, the portfolio is rebalanced. Generally, threshold-based rebalancing appears preferable because it makes moves when they are large enough to matter to the portfolio. This is shown in Figure 16.2, where the trades are denoted by the black circles and occur only when the asset moves significantly in price from its prior rebalance point. With period-based rebalancing there is a risk that a trade is unnecessary because the portfolio hasn't moved

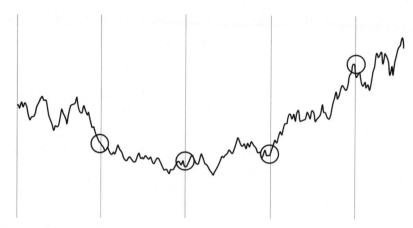

Figure 16.1   Time–Based Rebalancing
Source: FutureAdvisor modeling

much and any trading just drives up costs. For example, Hayne Leland at the University of California, Berkeley has found that, based on basic assumptions, time-based rebalancing can drive up transactions in a portfolio to double what they would be with threshold-based rebalancing without a material difference in tracking error.[3] That makes sense; if your portfolio is set up to rebalance once a quarter, then you'll get a rebalance once a quarter whether the market is virtually flat or experiencing the largest volatility in history. However, in those same environments, threshold-based rebalancing would avoid rebalancing in a virtually flat market and potentially rebalance more than once during a period of high volatility. With threshold-based rebalancing, a portfolio is rebalanced when it's most needed.

Figure 16.2   Threshold–Based Rebalancing
Source: FutureAdvisor modeling

Tiered Rebalancing

At FutureAdvisor, we go a step further with a tiered rebalancing approach. Different assets have different priorities for the portfolio, so drift in each asset carries differing costs for the portfolio. A deviation in the bond-equity split, for example, is likely to materially change the risk-reward profile of a portfolio, whereas a change in the allocation between U.S. stocks and U.S. value stocks has less significant portfolio impact because the U.S. stock market and U.S. value stocks have similar roles in the portfolio and performance is generally highly correlated between the asset classes. Therefore, it appears optimal to use threshold-based rebalancing but to implement it in a tiered fashion so that trades are made only when there is a deviation that matters at the level of portfolio construction. However, the need for rebalancing also interacts with other features of the algorithm in minimizing trading costs, so often rebalancing trades is combined with other trading goals, resulting in less portfolio turnover. For example, sometimes rebalancing can effectively be done for free if a tax loss harvesting trade is occurring or there is sufficient cash in the account to be invested and the algorithm can see those opportunities and take advantage of them.

Aside from helping align a portfolio with its long-term goals, if done correctly, rebalancing a portfolio has the potential to help performance, depending on the market environment. For example, David Swensen, manager of the Yale endowment and author of several portfolio management books found that rebalancing boosted returns between 1992 and 2002 by 0.4 percent a year based on Teachers Insurance and Annuity Association–College Retirement Equities Fund (TIAA-CREF) data. We should be careful here because the fundamental aim of rebalancing is to ensure that the portfolio meets its risk and return goals, rather than being a performance booster. Nonetheless, at certain times in the markets, rebalancing can be helpful to performance.

It is also worth taking a moment to consider what can happen to a portfolio in the absence of rebalancing. Unfortunately, this is an area where investors perform terribly. Without sound logic to guide asset allocation decisions, investors often tend to chase performance and move out of asset classes through fear at the wrong time. In academic terms we consider tiered threshold-based rebalancing against other rebalancing protocols. Yet, in real-world situations, rebalancing is compared against the behavior of the average investor, and the emotional factors at play here can be a real drag on returns. DALBAR studies of investor behavior have frequently identified investors' inability to time the market effectively, especially at times of high volatility, as the largest drag on investor performance. This can cost stock investors approximately 4 percent each year, depending on the time period.

Glidepaths

A second category of rebalancing helps maintain an appropriate portfolio as your needs change over time. This is commonly referred to as a glidepath. The term is borrowed from the technology that helps planes correctly judge their descent for landing, but is now heavily used in financial planning in relation to longer-term goals.

When you are young and investing for retirement you likely have decades before you need your retirement money. This is a great situation for an investor because, historically, if you have a very long time horizon, equities have generally done well, and even if there are falls in value—as inevitably happens—there's typically enough time that a good return will still be earned overall. For example, if you're 25 and planning to retire in your 60s, then an examination of historical market returns suggest that over four decades one can invest in the stock market with a high degree of confidence that the asset class will perform well relative to most others.

However, as retirement draws nearer, there's a need to be more cautious. If a market decline hits, then there may not be time to recover before the money is spent and the drawdown becomes permanent because spent money obviously can't be reinvested in the markets. For example, when you have a portfolio that is going to need to be spent in all or in part within 15 years, there are certainly historic scenarios where equity returns have been weak. Of course, you don't want to abandon equities entirely because there are equally as many scenarios when they have performed well over 15-year time horizons, but a greater weighting to fixed income and other assets becomes prudent to balance the risk of a bad stock scenario. Now, the logic at 15 years changes again as we get down to 10 years and so on. The same logic that enables you commit to the stock market for the long term starts to work in reverse. Your time horizon shortens, and as it does, you can no longer guarantee that stocks will come out ahead. As the odds change, your glidepath works to manage your portfolio risk year by year.

This is where a glidepath becomes helpful. Using various factors, but primarily your age, your allocation can be steadily adjusted downward as you age to best reflect the amount of risk your portfolio can tolerate.

Unlike rebalancing, this occurs not in reaction to market movements, but in reaction to changes in your own circumstances and the amount of risk your portfolio should be taking. Those saving early for retirement see little or no change in their allocation year to year. The difference between a 40- and a 39-year time horizon makes very little difference from a long-term standpoint—the prospects are good at 40 years to go and virtually identical at 39 years to go. However, as retirement gets to 15 years or less, market history suggests less certainty, so risk is correspondingly reduced.

As Robert Arnott of Research Affiliates has noted, effective glide paths should not just be characterized by their bond–equity split.[4] As we have discussed elsewhere, a well-balanced portfolio should take account of not just bond and equity exposure but the ability of subasset classes such as REITs within equities or Treasury inflation-protected securities (TIPS) within bonds to hedge inflation risk.

There is also a large amount of debate on the appropriate glidepath. The most obvious observation is that a 100 percent equity portfolio yields the highest returns in most historical assessments, especially for U.S. stocks. Of course, these data sets typically exclude China in 1947 and Russia in 1919, when equities fell to zero due to asset confiscation. There is general emphasis on the U.S. historical experience for modeling, which is something of a best-case example of what was an "emerging market" 100 years ago successfully emerging. Finally, though 100 percent equities may work for some, it is unlikely to work for all. A researcher can easily model out a 100 percent equity allocation, but it is much harder for a real investor to maintain it with a real portfolio. As we learned as recently as 2008, many investors will move to cash in the face of large market declines. We should also remember that your risk of losing your job can increase right at the point when stock markets are weakest. For example, the US Bureau of Labor Statistics estimates that 8 million jobs were lost during the 2007–2009 recession[5], when the markets also declined sharply. More generally, since 1945 1.5 percent to

10.1 percent of jobs have been lost during recessions, often with losses even higher in certain sectors such as manufacturing and technology. The fear of job loss may understandably decrease your ability to take on risk right when stocks are weakest. Therefore, 100 percent equities may be academically robust, but may carry greater risk than we capture in historical data sets, since it is not always implementable by the average person because of the increased risk of loss of employment income that can coincide with market declines.

Other glidepath shapes have been proposed: U shapes, inverted U shapes, and static allocations. However, behavioral finance has an important role to play here. Individuals are loss averse and not simply trying to maximize every last dollar for retirement. If you have $1 million, then the benefit of getting to $2 million is not the same as the cost of your nest egg falling to $0, even though both are a $1 million move in your portfolio and appear the same magnitude in dollar terms. As individuals approach retirement, they typically have a reasonable level of funds to meet their retirement goals, but not necessarily much more. This is where risk aversion comes in. Having more may be a nice to have, but having less would require cutbacks and be a major problem. Therefore, though some have proposed alternative glidepaths, and those may, in fact, result in higher total savings on average, the risk of having a lower standard of living in retirement should you get it wrong is pressing, and causes most to want to take a more protective approach when their retirement nest egg is close to being in place.

KEY TAKEAWAYS

- Rebalancing can help keep a portfolio aligned with its goals.
- Threshold-based rebalancing generally performs better than a period-based approach due to more efficient trading.
- Rebalancing may help returns in certain market environments, but the main value is in avoiding emotion based trades that can hurt performance.
- A glidepath can help manage the risk of a retirement portfolio over time, reducing risk as retirement draws closer.

Notes

1. Stewart A. Campbell, "Price Effects Surrounding Composition Changes of the S&P 500." Thesis, Stanford University, 2004.
2. Andrew Ang and Knut N. Kjaer, "Investing for the Long Run." Netspar Discussion Paper, January 2012.
3. Hayne Leland, "Optimal Portfolio Implementation with Transactions Costs and Capital Gains Taxes." Haas School of Business Technical Report, 2000.
4. Robert D. Arnott, Katrina F. Sherrerd, and Lillian Wu, "The Glidepath Illusion ... and Potential Solutions." *The Journal of Retirement* 1(2) (2013): 13–28.
5. Christopher J. Goodman and Steven M. Mance, "Employment Loss and the 2007-09 Recession: an Overview" *Monthly Labor Review*, April 2011: 3–12.

Chapter 17

How to Manage a Market Crash

"Never bet on the end of the world. It only happens once."

—Art Cashin

O ne reason to avoid the stock market is that it could crash overnight. Scary thought, no? In a similar way to plane crashes, market crashes are vivid events that scare us more than they should, statistically speaking, just as the drive to the airport is riskier than the flight. Figure 17.1 is an illustration of just how safe flying is compared to car travel. Fear and risk are quite different things.

In a similar manner, staying in cash, rather than being in stocks, can prove more costly to the growth of your savings than investing. Once again, the part of the human brain that was perfected to helping us avoid getting eaten by a tiger entices us to be scared into making poor

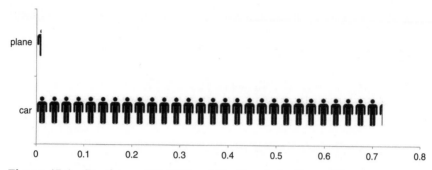

Figure 17.1   Deaths per 100 Million Miles Traveled—Car vs. Plane

financial decisions. We worry excessively about the big and scary—but unlikely—events, and this bias means that we end up overlooking the more mundane realities. The Standard & Poor's (S&P) 500 has fallen over 10 percent on 13 separate occasions in the past 70 years since the Second World War. That's roughly once every 6 years, but it's important to remember that on each occasions the market has come back to make new highs. In retrospect, that makes these declines look more like buying opportunities than risks for your investing strategy.

Figure 17.2 is a chart that shows for the S&P 500, going back almost 150 years, how long it would have taken you to get back to the same level after the various market declines.

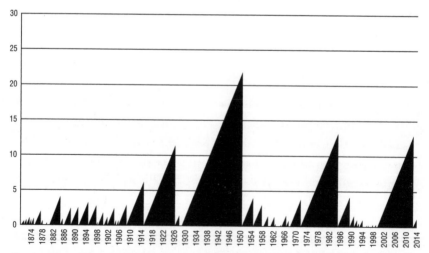

Figure 17.2   Recovery Time in Years from Historic S&P 500 Drawdowns: 1871–2014

Source: FutureAdvisor analysis.

For example, to take the biggest "triangle," if you'd bought stocks in September 1929 on the eve of the Great Depression when the S&P 500 was at 31, then you'd be waiting practically 25 years for the market to return to its prior level, which it ultimately did in September 1954.

Now, getting a little more sophisticated, we can adjust the data to include dividends and look at the real level of the index to take account of inflation. However, making these adjustments fails to alter the fundamental picture. With the exception of the Great Depression in the 1930s, you're looking at 15 years to make your money back if you happen to invest 100 percent of your money in U.S. stocks at four of the worst months to invest out of the last 1,716 (a 0.2 percent chance). Even altering the date you invest by a few months in these examples can improve the time it takes to break even by a few years, so you really do need exceptionally bad timing to experience the worst results. If you're saving money every few months, then it's highly unlikely you'd see results as bad as these because you'd still be contributing after the market fell and buying stocks at some of the most attractive values in history (of course, this was only apparent afterwards).

But let's not rely on luck, even though the odds are in our favor on this one. What are a few strategies we can use to minimize the risk still further?

Keep Stock Market Investing for Longer-Term Money

The first thing to take note of is that a majority stock portfolio is not for short-term investors. You want to have five years at a minimum until you need money that you're putting to work in the markets, and preferably longer. Otherwise, even a small disruption (such as the large number of smaller "triangles" on the chart in Figure 17.2) could force you to sell at precisely the time when you would want to be invested.

This means if you're young and saving for retirement, then a high allocation to stocks appears justified. However, if you're saving to purchase a house in 18 months' time, then having a large portion of that potential house down payment in stocks is likely to be too risky to meet your needs.

Making Saving an Ongoing Activity

The previous examples show the risk of putting 100 percent of your money in one asset class at a single point in time, and then failing to save any more. Ideally, you should save a proportion of your income every month. That's good financial practice in its own right, but it also means that your investment returns are likely to be smoother as you're slowly building an investments position over time by steady saving. If you're saving steadily over time, then you're more likely to achieve closer to the historical 7 percent long-term returns of the stock market rather than experiencing some of the more acute highs and lows.

Pay Attention to Extremes of Long-Term Valuation Signals

The Shiller cyclically adjusted price-to-earnings ratio (CAPE) can also be useful in this context. It's fairly complex, based on looking at stock prices relative to their earnings over the past decade. Doing so basically averages across the business cycle, so whether the current year is a good or bad one for the economy has limited impact on the valuation assessment. The underlying message is clear. Avoid being too heavily invested in stocks when valuations seem abnormally rich. This was particularly helpful in two instances in 1929 when the indicator was at 32× and in 1999 when it was at 43×. Its long-term average is 19×. It seems that as the CAPE metric rises, long-term returns over the next decade decline, and research supports this view, as Table 17.1 shows. That doesn't mean it's that helpful in the short term, but if you're looking ahead 10 years or more, then the CAPE can be useful. Also, note that even though CAPE is a relatively good indicator, it still leaves approximately 60 percent of future variation unexplained, so it's better than most indicators, yet still imprecise. Table 17.1 shows how historical CAPE ratios have been informative in predicting 10-year returns, but the maximum and minimum values also give an indication that the range of outcomes can be broad.

Table 17.1 U.S. 10-Year Returns Based on CAPE Values, 1881–2005

Shiller PE Value	Average 10-Year Annual Return	Maximum 10-Year Annual Return	Minimum 10-Year Annual Return
Under 12	7.6%	15.2%	−5.6%
Between 12 and 18	4.2%	16.6%	−4.9%
Over 18	2.5%	12.9%	−0.1%

Sources: Robert Shiller, FutureAdvisor

Don't Consider Stocks in Isolation

There is also no need to be 100 percent invested in U.S. stocks. Internationally diversifying your stock exposure can be helpful because the United States is less than a quarter of the global economy on most measures. Adding other developed markets can help spread risk, and adding emerging markets given demographic trends may help long-term returns. This is especially so in the current environment when the U.S. market appears relatively expensive by international standards, and looking overseas may help you find a better risk-return trade-off.

To find further balance it's important to consider adding some bonds and TIPS to your portfolio. These can do well at precisely the times stocks do poorly, so having at least 20 percent of your portfolio in these traditionally more stable instruments and growing their share as retirement approaches can help smooth out your returns when you need it most. There are other techniques to add portfolio balance, too. Real estate investment trusts (REITs) can help in certain market environments, and we believe tilts to value and smaller stocks can also boost returns based on Nobel Prize–winning research.

An example model portfolio to create balance that we use at FutureAdvisor is shown in Figure 17.3. Though this is just an example for those with several decades until retirement, your exact allocation should be adjusted to your age, retirement goal, and risk tolerance. The keys are to make sure you have a clear bond and equity split within your portfolio and diversify internationally.

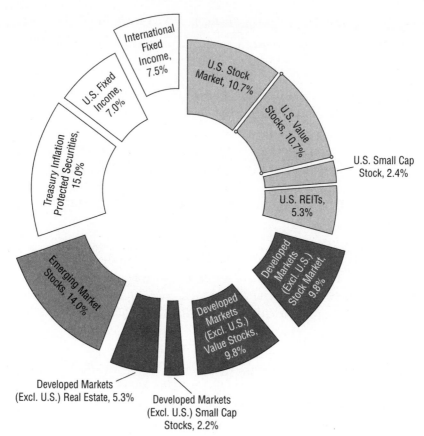

Figure 17.3   Example Portfolio Allocation
Source: FutureAdvisor

Remember that You May Underestimate Your Risk Tolerance in Good Markets

In good markets, fear of missing out can be a strong emotion. It can cause you to steadily increase the risk in your portfolio, but this risk typically comes with a larger downside if the markets do poorly. If the returns in bad markets are likely to make you change the course of your investment strategy, then that's a problem. Your investment strategy should be a reflection of your investment goals and not the market's performance. So when you're assessing your ability to manage risk, consider what actions you took during previous market downturns, or consider these historical performance numbers in bad markets. In the 1929 recession, the Dow fell 90 percent; over the course of the 1962 Cuban missile crisis, the Dow fell 27 percent, and it fell 30 percent during the 1970 recession and 45 percent during the 1973–1975 recession. More, recently the Dow fell 38 percent during the 2000–2001 recession and 50 percent during 2008–2009. Of course, every recession is unique in some way, but it's clear that double-digit stock market declines are reasonably common. Portfolio diversification can provide some moderation here, and in all these cases, the market went on to once again hit new highs, but your ability to stay the course through whatever market turmoil occurs in the future is important for your financial success. If not, you are likely going to achieve better returns through a conservative strategy that you can apply consistently.

KEY TAKEAWAYS

- Longer-term investors worry about market crashes more than they should. They are relatively infrequent, and investors with long-term horizons are better accepting that crashes will occur rather than trying to avoid them by staying in cash.
- Ongoing saving can help to smooth your returns and reduce the impact of any extreme market event.
- Paying attention to long-term valuation signals and diversifying internationally and by asset class can be helpful.
- Ultimately, picking a plan you can stick with in bad markets is crucial. Needing to sell in a bear market, can be harmful to long-term returns.

Chapter 18

Your Own Worst Enemy Is in the Mirror

"The key to making money in stocks is not to get scared out of them."

—Peter Lynch

Most people know how they should invest, but few actually do so. Behaving rationally is hard when it's your money at stake and especially when you're losing it. Even though these short-term losses are typically temporary in the context of a broader strategy, that doesn't make it any easier when it's happening.

The Biggest Threat to Your Returns
Is in the Mirror

One of the biggest problems for investors is market timing. This means taking a view on which way the market is going to move next. The basic problem is that market timing can leave you out of the market when it is rising in value and be a drag on performance. The trade to exit is fairly easy. You worry about something bad that will happen or see a large price fall and you sell your shares. The problem is that getting back in is harder. Emotionally, you want the trade to work, so you are tempted to stay out of the market waiting for a move down if one doesn't happen.

The reverse problem occurs as markets rise. It can be easy to stay the course when the market is rising. In fact, it seems so easy that you believe you have more risk tolerance than you actually do. Risk tolerance is hard to truly measure until the markets are falling. Fear of missing out on returns starts to drive your behavior; you check your portfolio more frequently and are tempted to do more short-term trades. Since the market is generally rising, it becomes easier to make money. Even a trade that lags the market's return and would lose you money in a flat or down market becomes tempting in a bull market because it appears superficially profitable. As investors, we tend to focus on the basis result of whether an investment went up or down, rather than a more appropriate analysis of how it did relative to a benchmark after costs. Because of this, any activity in a bull market looks good. Just as during the stock boom of the late 1990s, many people convinced themselves that they were successful day traders, moving in and out of stocks within a single day and making money. It was relatively easy to do this when the Standard & Poor's (S&P) 500 returned more than 20 percent every single year between 1995 and 1999. Even a trade that lost 15 percent relative to the market would still appear profitable because the market was rising so drastically. Of course, the next three years of negative returns taught day traders otherwise, and what had seemed like a profitable endeavor wasn't.

As Warren Buffett has said, "Only when the tide goes out do you discover who's been swimming naked." What he means is that certain financial practices show their limitations only in weaker markets, and this problem is compounded in that the investing tide doesn't come in and out every day. In the 1980s and 1990s, the market rose for eight and nine years, respectively, without seeing an annual decline, though the average is about three years, looking back over this century. People generally respond well to feedback, but unfortunately the markets can take years to provide feedback on whether a strategy is valuable for the longer term, and short-term performance can be misleading.

Always a Reason to Avoid Staying Out

Equally, there are always reasons to avoid the stock market; for example, let's look at 2013. This was a year when the federal government was shut down for 16 days in October, and major terrorist attacks happened at both the Boston marathon and a Kenyan shopping mall. A typhoon killed thousands in the Philippines. Egypt was plunged into turmoil after its leader was ousted. JPMorgan paid one of the largest fines on record, and Edward Snowden disclosed many details about government surveillance that caused international uproar. Of course, 2013 is not unique in this regard. Bad events occur continually, but for someone trying to time the market, it's never hard to find a reason to delay getting back in. How did the S&P 500 perform in 2013? Well, for all those terrible events, it rose over 32 percent on a total return basis. The point is not that bad events cause the market to rise; it's that the global picture is always mixed. Whatever the market environment, there is always bad news to be found.

The DALBAR study of mutual fund investor behavior has shown that investors often exit the market at times of high volatility and do not reenter the market as quickly as they should. Since over time the market has historically risen, this approach of balancing being in and out of the market tends to cost in returns.

The Returns You See Aren't the Ones You Get after Tax

Market timing also comes with tax inefficiency. If you are trading positions, then you may end up holding them for under a year. Under the current tax code for most investors, holding something for less than a year can increase the tax cost of the position.

The tax code will change over time, but assume that you pay tax of 35 percent on short-term gains, and 20 percent on long-term gains. If you fortunately have an investment that's up 20 percent over six months, then your post-tax return would be 13 percent if you held it for less than a year, but 16 percent if you held it for over a year. In fact, the investment could even fall in value by over 3 percent and you'd still make more money after tax waiting for it to be a long-term capital gain. Given that over time, stocks tend to rise in value, selling something that's made a profit within a year is very often a losing proposition. The problem is that market timing can often push you into shorter holding periods.

Of course, the problem is that investors and the media spend most of the time looking at pretax numbers. It's somewhat inevitable—everyone's tax situation is different, and some accounts pay no tax at all or defer it far into the future. However, the shortcut of looking at pretax returns means that investors aren't as focused on tax efficiency as they should be.

The Media Isn't Your Friend

The media isn't always the treasure trove of information to the investor that it may appear. For example, the market making new highs often gets headlines, but since 1950 the U.S. market has made a monthly new high one month in four on average. The media has to produce stories every day, even if there is no real news. Reading it can cause you to want to take action and make trades in your portfolio, but often this is counterproductive.

Overtrading

Another problem that can result from market timing is overtrading. As much as fees have fallen, commissions, bid-ask spreads, and even the impact of being in the market and changing prices can be a drag on returns. The more often you trade, the more often you incur these costs, dragging down your returns. Let's assume you have a portfolio of 20 $5,000 positions. You pay $5 for each trade (both the buy and sell, so $10 total) and 0.1 percent in bid-ask spreads. That's a 0.3 percent cost every time you trade. So if you trade every position every three months, you are paying 1.2 percent a year in extra fees, whereas if you hold every position for 10 years, then your trading cost on an annual basis is just

0.03 percent. Again, it can be tempting to trade, but the expected returns from a portfolio trade are always uncertain, but the cost is always there and can be a significant drag on returns, as you may have noticed in the example above.

Research has shown just how hard it is for people to do nothing even when the cost of action can be harmful. Neuroscientists at the University of Virginia and Harvard found that rather than sit and do nothing for up to 15 minutes, many people would actually give themselves electric shocks rather than endure doing nothing.[1] If you're a man you are more likely to suffer from this problem, almost two thirds of men in the study chose the electric shock but only one in four women did.

Home Bias

A big issue for investors that still hasn't gone away is home bias. Investors tend to hold what they know. Holding stock in your employer is perhaps the worst example here. Your salary, bonus, and indeed your job security are directly linked to the stock price of your employer, and yet many people have their employer's firm as the largest stock in their portfolio. Sometimes, there are reasons for this such as attractive stock purchase plans or tax considerations, but generally people should be wary of employer stock.

A second issue occurs with international investing. The numbers on domestic stock holdings are quite surprising. The efficient portfolio for someone in the United States, Europe, or Asia is not that different. Yet if you look at actual portfolios, domestic stocks always dominate. This means people are giving up an efficient investment approach to hold what they know, and the costs can be significant. This effect has diminished over time, but it is still present.

Failing to Take a Long-Term Perspective

If you're in your 20s or 30s and saving for retirement, then you have decades ahead of you. However, it can be tempting to take a shorter-term view, not investing today because the outlook is bad or there's something to worry about this week or month. However, this inaction overlooks the issue that for the long term you do want to be invested. Delaying or trading in and out typically harms returns.

Availability Bias

Humans are very good at focusing on recent history. People worry more about plane crashes when there has been one in the news. Similarly, people worry about market crashes when one has recently happened. Ironically, this can produce the opposite of correct behavior. Typically, the market's falling can make it cheaper. Often, declines do not coincide with as great a fall in expected long-term earnings of the market, so after a crash, the markets may represent *better* value than previously. However, the tendency is to look back at what has recently happened, rather than forward at what might happen given past events.

Chasing Performance

Just as fear of losing money is a big driver of raw investor emotion, so fear of missing out on gains can also drive investor actions. It can be tempting to purchase a "hot" mutual fund because of strong recent results. Research has shown that fees and investment mandate can predict mutual fund performance, but that evidence for managers being sustainably better than average is not clear. There is some evidence that exceptionally bad performance can persist, so if a mutual fund has terrible performance, that could be a bad sign, but great performance is not necessarily a great sign for future years. There is some evidence that stocks that do well can continue to do well for periods of less than a year, but this doesn't necessarily translate into superior mutual fund performance.

Ignoring Fees

Related to the issue of performance is the issue of fees. It turns out that fees are a generally good predictor of performance. This isn't that surprising if manager skill is random. For example, a fund with a 3 percent fee will perform worse than underperform a fund with a no fee all else equal by 3 percent a year. Basically, the issue with mutual funds is not that they are inherently bad, but they can never overcome the considerable handicap of their fees. They are generally neutral in performance relative to the market, which is exactly what you would expect because when you combine all the participants in the market, you will receive the market return, but fees do create a drag on performance.

Holding Too Much Cash

Cash is the ultimate way to slowly lose money. Inflation is generally positive, so each year a dollar buys you less. Like investment fees, the amount each year can be small, but over time it adds up. With just 2 percent inflation a year, the purchasing power of your money halves over 35 years. And remember, compounding works the other way, too; if you can earn a return of 6 percent a year, your money will double in 12 years. So cash is often a disappointment in its own right, but becomes even more so when you consider the other ways you can be investing your money. Yes, but it's safe, you might argue. There's some truth to that. There have been a handful of years this century when both stocks and bonds have lost money over the course of a year, but they are relatively rare, and, of course, cash is certain to lose money in the presence of inflation.

How Software Can Help

There is an opportunity for digital advisors to help with this problem based on the detailed level of customization that can be provided. For example, it's possible to send tailored messages to customers who check performance too often, reminding them that checking performance daily for a long-term portfolio is probably a waste of effort. It's also possible to show very detailed and personalized explanations to clients on every trade that was made and the rationale, every tax loss harvest that occurred, and the rationale for specific selections in their portfolio. Such detailed communication is possible because of software that can determine the relevant message to display to each customer, creating a uniquely personalized experience based on scalable infrastructure.

Digital portfolio management also enables the use of "good defaults" in maintaining portfolios. Rather than having to actively make a decision during a bad market environment when fear is present and emotion is high, a digital approach can use an algorithm to automatically make rebalancing trades that are grounded in research. These trades can be made automatically, rather than requiring an explicit decision process from the investor at times of potential high panic and stress, which is exactly when human decision making can perform poorly.

KEY TAKEAWAYS

- Rational behavior is easy in theory, but challenging when it's your money on the line.
- It's important to stick to your plan, but the media and the way our brains work make it tempting to change course even when it's not potentially costly.
- Chasing performance, ignoring fees, and holding too much in stocks or countries we know can also hinder performance.
- Software can help maintain a robust plan and share timely information on what's being done and why it's useful.

Note

1. T. D. Wilson, D. A. Reinhard, E. C. Westgate, and D. T. Gilbert, "Which Would You Prefer—Do Nothing or Receive Electric Shocks?" Science 345 no. 6192 (2014) 75-77.

Chapter 19

Saving for Goals
beyond Retirement

"An investor without investment objectives is like a traveler
without a destination."

—Ralph Seger

Retirement is a critical goal to save for. It's often said that you
cannot borrow to fund your retirement. This is true in contrast
to other savings goals, such as funding college for children,
where it's quite possible to borrow funds if needed to cover the expense.
Of course, some other savings goals can be cut entirely. You can decide
not to remodel the bathroom, but most cannot decide not to retire.

As such, it's important to make sure that you are broadly on track for
retirement before saving for other goals that are likely less important from
a lifetime standpoint. Table 19.1 gives an approximate sense of how your
savings should compare with your salary based on your age if you're on

Table 19.1   Assessing Your Saving for Retirement as a Multiple of Salary

Age	Retirement Savings as Proportion of Salary—Relaxed Assumptions	Retirement Savings as Proportion of Salary—Strict Assumptions
30	0.5×	2×
35	0.7×	3×
40	1×	4×
45	2.5×	5×
50	2.5×	6×
55	3.5×	8×
60	5×	10×
65	7×	13×

Source: FutureAdvisor analysis.

track with retirement saving. There are two columns—the right assumes a better rate of return in the markets, lower life expectancy, and a higher savings rate. The left assumes a lower market return, longer life expectancy, and lower savings rate. It's helpful to think about savings within a range rather than an absolute firm value because there are a number of uncertainties in creating the correct forecast for any individual.

Ideally, you want to have saved at least the multiple of salary shown in the left column depending on your age, and if you're close to the multiple in the right column then you appear well on track, even if you live much longer than average or market returns are unexpectedly very poor.

Tax Efficiency

It may not surprise you to hear that tax efficiency is an important concern when saving for goals beyond retirement, just as it is for retirement. Table 19.2 details some of the options depending on what you are saving for.

College savings has various tax-efficient options for savings. The most common are 529 plans, and Coverdell education savings accounts (ESAs) can be a good option for those on relatively low income. Also, in certain circumstances, a trust may be helpful for college saving for wealthier families, though the tax benefits are generally less.

Though 529s and Coverdell ESAs are generally two of the better ways to save for college, it's also worth noting that individual retirement accounts (IRAs) can be used to fund certain higher education expenses.

Table 19.2   Tax Efficiency for Goals beyond Retirement

Goal/Need	Tax Efficient Options
College and further education	529, Coverdell ESA, IRA
Medical expenses	IRA, 401(k)
First home deposit	IRA
Health insurance if unemployed	IRA

Source: FutureAdvisor analysis

There's also a little-known tax-advantaged way to save for your first home using an IRA. You can take $10,000 from an IRA to fund a first home without penalty, provided you have saved the money for at least five years. However, doing this also reduces the funds you are able to tax shelter for retirement if you are already maxing out your IRA contributions.

Finally, though not a savings goal, IRAs can also play a role as a sort of emergency fund in certain scenarios. For example, in the event of a permanent disability, an IRA can be accessible without penalty. Certain large medical costs can also be funded from 401(k)s and IRAs, and your medical costs can be paid from an IRA if you're employed. Clearly, these scenarios aren't as flexible as a true emergency fund in covering rent if you lose your job temporarily, but they do offer some flexibility for some of life's unexpected hardships.

So tax shelters shouldn't be thought of only in saving for retirement costs. Education, medical costs, and a first home can all be areas where tax shelters apply.

Portfolio Construction

For goals other than retirement, time horizons are typically shorter, and this changes the investment allocation. For retirement, as discussed in earlier chapters, history strongly suggests that if you are investing for a long enough period, a bad market can be endured and returns should ultimately be positive. This leads to high confidence in large stock allocation for younger investors. However, for shorter time horizons, the risks of the market increase because there may be insufficient time to recover from a market drawdown. This leads to a lower weighting to stocks relative to bonds. The result is that the portfolio is more robust in bad markets, though this comes at the cost of lower expected returns.

Emergency Funds

In addition to focusing on future goals (whatever they may be), managing financial risks is also important. That's why an emergency fund should be kept on hand to deal with short-term problems such as losing your job. This fund should enable you to keep up with expenses such as rent while you find a new source of income. Of course, investment funds may also be used for this purpose, but there's the risk of having to sell into a bad market, or having to take a financial penalty to withdraw from a tax shelter. Although cash will lose money over time, having some cash investment can be useful for a short-term emergency fund so it's always there when and if you need it. Typically, three to nine months of expenditure represents an appropriate emergency fund for most.

Investment Flow Chart

Of course, keeping all these different goals and priorities straight can be a challenge. Figure 19.1 can help you perform a rough assessment of your priorities for where you next investment dollar should be headed.

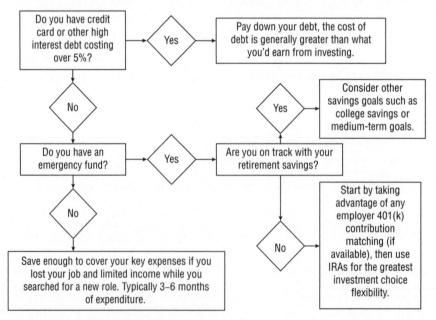

Figure 19.1 Savings Flowchart

Source: FutureAdvisor analysis.

KEY TAKEAWAYS

- Retirement isn't the only investment goal, but it is the most important. Consider other goals only once your retirement savings is on track.
- An emergency fund is an important way to manage the expenses associated with losing your job or another emergency. So keeping cash on hand for that is a smart strategy if it hinders your returns.
- Other goals beyond retirement can have tax incentives, so be aware of your options, as these can boost your after-tax returns. Examples include saving for education or a first home.
- How you allocate a portfolio for other goals should depend primarily on your time horizon. The further out you need the money, the greater weight you can place on stocks.

Chapter 20

A History of Diversified Portfolio Performance

"That men do not learn very much from the lessons of history
is the most important of all the lessons of history."

—Aldous Huxley

I n looking forward to estimate future returns, it can be helpful to
look back. History is a useful guide in assessing future scenarios and
risk factors for portfolios.

Stocks vs. Bonds

Table 20.1 reveals some fundamental points about stocks and bonds.
Stocks have a broader range of returns than bonds do, but bond returns
are less likely to be negative. The data also reinforce the point that over

Table 20.1   Historical U.S. Nominal Returns

Decade	Average Annual Stock Return	Average Annual 10-Year Bond Return
1930s	−1%	4%
1940s	9%	3%
1950s	19%	1%
1960s	8%	2%
1970s	6%	5%
1980s	17%	12%
1990s	18%	7%
2000s	−1%	6%

Source: FutureAdvisor

long time periods, stocks are less risky than they appear in the short term. The only exception to that would be China and Russia, where asset confiscation led to complete losses at periods in the twentieth century, but otherwise this assumption holds across geographies.

Also, note that stocks outperform bonds in most environments except where stocks experience absolute declines, which becomes less common as you extend your investment horizon. This is as expected, given that stocks are well positioned to benefit from economic growth, whereas bond returns are typically limited by fixed nominal coupon payments if held to maturity.

The Impact of Recessions

The 1930s and 2000s both show how recession can drag down stock returns. In the 1930s, weak growth and limited policy responses caused significant market declines both early and late in the decade. In the 2000s, the timing is somewhat unfortunate in that the decade begins with the bursting of the tech bubble and then ends in a relatively deep recession. However, it is reassuring that these two bad decades see only minor stock declines for the decade in aggregate, and in both cases expanding the time period just one year returns the index to positive returns.

The Impact of Inflation

The oil price shock in the 1970s led to high inflation. By the early 1980s, inflation hit 14 percent, which might seem unthinkable today. Inflation is dangerous to portfolios because it can reduce returns on both stocks and bonds. This is why it is helpful to include potential inflation hedges in the portfolio such as real estate investment trusts (REITs) and Treasury inflation-protected securities (TIPS).

However, the 1980s clearly demonstrate the positive impact of falling inflation. Paul Volcker at the Federal Reserve aggressively targeted inflation, causing two recessions in the process, but the impact on the markets was positive, since inflation is so critical in determining asset values and lower inflation increases the value of return returns. Thus, falling inflation made the 1980s one of the best decades for investors.

The Danger of Averages

The decade-based data also highlight the risk of relying on average returns as a guide. Though bonds have delivered single-digit returns relatively consistently through decades and have never deviated too far from the period average of 5 percent, the picture for equities is far more ambiguous, with broad swings from a positive return of 19 percent to a loss of 1 percent in two separate decades.

The Benefits of Combination

The data also show why stocks and bonds are so useful in combination. A combination of the asset classes had the potential to avoid negative returns in both the 1930s and 2000s. Though it's also clear that this smoothness in returns comes at a cost, since the returns to bonds are lower, adding them to the portfolio reduces the risk of loss in any decade but also lowers return, particularly in the 1950s and 1990s. Of course, this assumes that you remain invested through the highs and lows, and we should not forget that one advantage of a portfolio is in enabling you to stay the course with an investment strategy. Though its easy to take this for granted, the benefits of implementing an investment strategy consistently can be material, and, of course, as countless market declines have shown, many overstate their ability to stay the course.

An Emerging Market that Has Emerged

The U.S. data shown benefits from looking at the United States essentially as an emerging market that has emerged over time into a position of relative political and economic dominance. In the 1930s, America's place in the world was not well defined, and by the turn of the millennium, it was preeminent. This ascent has been a benefit for trade and the financial markets of the United States as a result. Analysis of other countries shows that the United States falls at the high end of potential outcomes in terms of financial market experiences over the past century.

KEY TAKEAWAYS

- Stock returns have historically been higher but more volatile than returns for bonds.
- The weakest decades for stocks involved multiple recessions or unanticipated inflation.
- Generally, stocks outperform bonds over long time periods.

Chapter 21

The Future of Wealth Management

"Prediction is very difficult, especially about the future."

—Niels Bohr

T he so-called FinTech industry has shown rapid growth in just a handful of years. Innovation is a powerful force, and many of the trends that have been true even before the onset of digital innovation are set to continue. In assessing the future direction of the industry, it is helpful to look back rather than forward because some of the most powerful trends we have seen continually in the past will likely have a significant impact on the future.

Lower Costs

Charles Jones of Columbia Business School has performed extensive research on trading costs[1] and found that they have halved every seven to eight years since 1976. For example, New York Stock Exchange commissions during the 1960s had the structure shown in Table 21.1.

Also, remember that the costs in Table 21.1 are not adjusted for inflation—that $39 fee from the 1960s would be $270 in 2015 dollars. As such, the decline in commissions is stark. With trades possible today at a cost of $7, that's less than 3 percent of the cost of the 1960s in real terms.

For comparison, many popular exchange-traded funds (ETFs) now trade commission free at major brokerages. Similar trends are evident in ETF expense ratios, mutual fund load fees, and bid-ask spreads. Everywhere, costs are falling and continue to fall. This decline has also been met with an increase in trading volume, as you would expect. When something is cheaper, people tend to buy more of it. Though costs are now at relatively low levels, the decline in costs has shown no signs of abating. It is reasonable to expect this trend of falling costs to continue and benefit investors in two ways: first, in lowering direct costs, but second and perhaps more importantly, in opening up financial services to those with smaller account balances.

Remember that declining costs are not necessarily bad for the wealth management industry. Even today, only a minority of households receive professional financial advice, so with declining costs there is ample opportunity for the industry to expand significantly. This also suggests that the typical assumption that digital advisors will replace incumbent firms is exaggerated, largely because the main opportunity for digital advisors is in opening up investment advice to households that currently have none, rather than targeting existing clients of other firms.

Table 21.1   NYSE Trading Commissions 1959–1968

Money Involved	Minimum Commission per 100 Shares
$100 to $400	$3 + 2% of amount traded ($6 minimum)
$400 to $2,400	$7 + 1% of amount traded
$2,400 to $5,000	$19 + 0.5% of amount traded
Over $5,000	$39 + 0.1% of amount traded

Source: Charles Jones

An important additional gain from declining costs is increased innovation. Recall that many of the portfolio tilts we discussed previously make sense on paper without consideration of implementation costs but fail to deliver value once costs are considered. Declining costs opens the door for greater innovation in portfolio construction, since the market is generally efficient and gains from any strategy are often relatively small. Declining costs lowers the bar for effective strategies to become profitable, and hence has the potential to encourage innovation in portfolio construction.

There is also an open question about whether as many of the transactional costs of portfolio implementation decline to very low levels and whether tax costs will assume greater prominence in reporting and day-to-day investment discussions. Today, tax topics are underrepresented relative to the drag that they create on portfolio returns. Improvement in messaging and reporting of the tax efficiencies offered by digital services is a possible next step, though it remains challenging to educate clients on a dry topic, albeit one that can substantially help returns.

Democratization of Services

Previously, advanced techniques such as tax loss harvesting, automated rebalancing, and tax-efficient asset placement were the preserve of wealthy investors. Given the human effort involved in these tasks, the payoff wasn't worth it for the smaller client. The costs were largely fixed and didn't exceed the benefits. Algorithms have irreversibly changed these economics. Regardless of how complex the rules, algorithms have an edge over humans for known and repeatable problems. Over time, wealth management services will offer further sophistication even for the youngest clients, given that algorithms change the economics of service provision. What is available to one is now cheaply and easily available to all.

One obvious example of this is expansion of services. For example, FutureAdvisor was founded on retirement planning but has rapidly expanded to encompass other relevant investment goals for the household such as college savings. The broadening scope of digital investment management is likely to continue, with the initial focus being understandably on the broadest opportunities but niche and important areas attracting greater coverage over time.

Increasing Customer Intimacy

With the increasing acceptance of behavioral finance, and the recognition that individuals all learn and make decisions in slightly different ways, there is an opportunity for the wealth management industry to offer ever greater customization to clients, what Harvard professor Michael Porter terms customer intimacy. Today, this is a reality at the portfolio level, where myriad client circumstances lead to a portfolio that is truly unique based on unique client circumstances and portfolio tax factors, despite being drawn from a consistent set of market assumptions. Messaging around that portfolio is becoming increasingly customized.

Messaging may seem trivial compared to portfolio construction, but research suggests that the challenge of investors staying the course in adhering to a given strategy is just as important as the strategy itself. During buoyant markets, the issue is hidden, but research suggests that in down markets, the costs to clients of switching strategies can materially hurt returns. Hence, improvements in educating clients about the unique circumstances of their portfolio and providing timely and personalized content based on their needs is readily achievable and no more than the expansion of the techniques already successfully implemented in portfolio management, just applied to a different problem.

Improved Financial Awareness

Less a prediction than a need, there also needs to be an improved understanding across society of the importance of investing. With the onus on individuals to largely now provide for their own retirement, rather than rely on their employer, the understanding of households of good investment practices has not kept pace with the need for them, and financial planning remains largely absent from school curricula despite its fundamental importance in life.

Previously, as discussed from a cost standpoint, it simply was too expensive for individuals to engage with a financial advisor and learn the concepts needed to succeed in meeting investment goals, but the onset of digital investment management has changed that equation and should lead to improved financial "literacy" among the population.

KEY TAKEAWAYS

- Just as predictions in the stock market are challenging, so predictions about the industry should be taken with some skepticism.
- Falling costs for investors have been a broad trend that looks likely to continue.
- Services previously offered only to the wealthiest will increasingly be offered broadly through software.
- Software will also get ever better at offering a completely unique experience for every customer, from investment policy to communications.

Note

1. Charles M. Jones, "A Century of Stock Market Liquidity and Trading Costs." Columbia University, May 23, 2002.

Chapter 22

Conclusion

A key message is that in constructing and maintaining a portfolio, many factors should be considered in parallel, and asset allocation is just one part of the puzzle. Humans don't do well with a large array of diverse and ever-changing inputs. Fortunately, algorithms are able to excel at this. Asset class selection gets a lot of the attention in investment writing and analysis. Rightly so, since it's critical to success and to the extent that the period from the 1970s and 2010s has been relatively benign for investors due to falling inflation, the coming decades may offer a greater challenge. However, fees, trading costs, and taxes are equally important, and a portfolio that might appear optimal from an asset allocation standpoint can fall behind due to these hidden costs, which often aren't on investors' radars. It's only when a portfolio is considered after all costs that the optimal solution can be found.

For example, consider Warren Buffett, almost certainly one of the greatest investors of all time. Even he may be having trouble in recent years matching his past performance. Through 2014 the growth in the book value of his company beat the Standard & Poor's (S&P) 500 by an average of 9.5 percent a year. If you have one of the best investment records on the planet, that is just about the best you can reasonably hope for, during what was also, historically speaking, a pretty good period to be an investor due to generally declining inflation, favorable demographics, and increasing global development and trade and no large-scale global military conflicts. So Buffett is an astute investor and also had the advantage of investing during a relatively favorable period.

Let's assume we get that stellar return and beat the market by 9.5 percent a year. Surprisingly, if we don't focus on the details of cost and taxes, we can actually end up lagging the market. Let's work through how that can happen.

Assume that you don't focus on taxes. You sell everything in under a year rather than holding it for as long as reasonably possible. Depending on your tax bracket and state, a household could end up paying 33 percent a year on investment gains rather than potentially 0 percent by implementing a tax-efficient buy-and-hold strategy and assuming tax shelters appropriately. In the Warren Buffett example, his annual return was 19.4 percent, so capital gains taxes could take 6.4 percent off that. That's a big hit.

Morningstar reported that in 2014 the average mutual fund cost 1.25 percent a year. Yet exchange-traded funds (ETFs) can now track the U.S. stock market with high accuracy, liquidity, tax efficiency, and low bid-ask spreads for 0.04 percent. So the cost of picking the wrong fund can be 1.21 percent a year, even today in a world where fund costs have declined considerably. Of course, Buffett's not picking mutual funds, but many investors are, so even though it doesn't matter for Buffett, it probably does matter for you.

Then assume inefficiency in turnover relating to trading. Picking funds with high bid-ask spreads can drive up the total cost of a trade by 0.3 percent. Paying commissions when commission-free options are available can again cost you 0.3 percent on a small position, so that's 0.6 percent due to inefficient trading, assuming you turn over your portfolio once a year, which is consistent with our prior assumption of short-term capital gains.

Finally, tax loss harvesting can be implemented in any taxable portfolio and offer gains of around 1 percent, depending on the composition of the portfolio and the market environment.

So we have 6.4 percent lost in taxes, 1.2 percent lost in fees, 0.6 percent on direct and indirect trading costs, and a potential 1 percent gain from deciding to implement tax loss harvesting. That's a 9.6 percent change in performance completely independent of investment selection, rebalancing, and performance. Remember, Warren Buffett beat the S&P 500 by 9.5 percent annually, so a sloppy approach to tax, fees, and trading has the potential to remove more than his entire investment acumen.

I'm sure Warren Buffett is very smart about these other aspects, too, of course, but how many media articles have you read about great investors minimizing taxable gains or focusing on bid-ask spreads? I suspect it's exactly zero. I'm not saying they'd make for great reading, but it does make an impressive difference on returns.

Now, consider the reverse. It's basically impossible to replicate Buffett's returns. Many have tried; no one has succeeded. Even Buffett's own recent returns now lag his historical performance (though his business is much larger now than it was). Compared to that, consider how much easier it is to run a portfolio that is low cost, tax efficient, and smart about trading costs. The point is that those are things that you can control, and the impact on your returns has about the same impact as achieving one of the best portfolios in history.

Of course, the pundits will continue to focus on the asset allocation decision. It's a fascinating and ever-changing world with millions of inputs and enormous complexity, but the more pedestrian side of taxes, fees, and costs may be less exciting and can do just as much good for your portfolio. As such, the digital investment space has a bright future.

Yet, none of this technology matters if you fail to save enough. The biggest step you can take to reach your savings goals is to increase your savings rate today.

Author's Disclaimer

The views expressed herein are those of the author and are not those of FutureAdvisor and its affiliates (collectively, "FutureAdvisor") or the publisher. Neither FutureAdvisor nor the publisher endorses or approves the views in this book. Nothing contained herein is intended to serve as a forecast, a guarantee of future results, investment recommendations, or an offer to buy or sell securities by FutureAdvisor or the publisher. The investment strategies mentioned are not personalized to your financial circumstances or investment objectives. Differences in account size, timing of transactions, and market conditions prevailing at the time of investment may lead to different results, and you may lose money.

Past performance is not indicative of future results. Hypothetical performance (such as back tested results or projected performance) does not reflect the performance of actual accounts and is not a guarantee of future results. The tax strategies discussed, including tax loss harvesting, should not be interpreted as tax advice, and FutureAdvisor does not represent in any manner that the tax consequences detailed will be obtained or that any tax strategy will result in any particular tax consequence. You should consult with your personal tax advisors regarding the tax consequences of investing.

Limit of Liability/Disclaimer of Warranty: The publisher and the author make no representations or warranties with respect to the accuracy or completeness of the contents of this work and specifically disclaim all warranties, including without limitation warranties of fitness for a particular purpose. No warranty may be created or extended by sales or promotional materials. The advice and strategies contained herein may not be suitable for every situation. This work is sold with the understanding that the publisher is not engaged in rendering legal, accounting, or other professional services. If professional assistance is required, the services of a competent professional person should be sought. Neither the publisher nor the author shall be liable for damages arising here from. The fact that an organization or web site is referred to in this work as a citation and/or a potential source of further information does not mean that the author or the publisher endorses the information the organization or web site may provide or recommendations it may make. Further, readers should be aware that Internet web sites listed in this work may have changed or disappeared between when this work was written and when it is read.

About the Author

S imon Moore is chief investment officer at FutureAdvisor, where he oversees the investment process and tenets of the digital investment manager. He is a Chartered Financial Analyst charterholder, with an economics degree from Oxford University and an MBA from Northwestern University's Kellogg School of Management. Simon previously worked for Putnam Investments, Microsoft, and the Bank of England. He regularly writes about and comments on savings and investment topics for outlets including *Forbes,* CNN, and the *Huffington Post.* He previously wrote *Strategic Project Portfolio Management* (Wiley, 2009). He grew up in Britain and now lives in the United States with his wife and two children.

Index